Pope
Benedict
XVI

Other books in the People in the News series:

David Beckham
Beyoncé
Kelly Clarkson
Hillary Clinton
Hilary Duff
Zac Efron
50 Cent
Tony Hawk
LeBron James
Angelina Jolie
Ashton Kutcher
Tobey Maguire
John McCain
Barack Obama
Queen Latifah
Condoleezza Rice
J.K. Rowling
Shakira
Tupac Shakur
Ben Stiller
Hilary Swank
Justin Timberlake
Usher

Pope Benedict XVI

by Barbara Sheen

LUCENT BOOKS

A part of Gale, Cengage Learning

GALE
CENGAGE Learning™

Detroit • New York • San Francisco • New Haven, Conn • Waterville, Maine • London

LIBRARY OF CONGRESS CATALOGING-IN-PUBLICATION DATA

Sheen, Barbara.
  Pope Benedict XVI / by Barbara Sheen.
    p. cm. — (People in the news)
  Includes bibliographical references and index.
  ISBN 978-1-4205-0093-6 (hardcover)
  1. Benedict XVI, Pope, 1927- 2. Popes—Biography. I. Title.
  BX1378.6.S54 2009
  282.092—dc22
  [B]
                                                        2008025634

Lucent Books
27500 Drake Rd
Farmington Hills MI 48331

ISBN-13: 978-1-4205-0093-6
ISBN-10: 1-4205-0093-7

Printed in the United States of America
1 2 3 4 5 6 7 12 11 10 09 08

Contents

Foreword   6

Introduction   8
A New Pope

Chapter 1   14
Church and Family

Chapter 2   28
A Reluctant Warrior

Chapter 3   42
Priest and Scholar

Chapter 4   59
Protector of the Faith

Chapter 5   75
Facing the Future

Notes   90

Important Dates   94

For More Information   97

Index   99

Picture Credits   104

About the Author   104

Fame and celebrity are alluring. People are drawn to those who walk in fame's spotlight, whether they are known for great accomplishments or for notorious deeds. The lives of the famous pique public interest and attract attention, perhaps because their experiences seem in some ways so different from, yet in other ways so similar to, our own.

Newspapers, magazines, and television regularly capitalize on this fascination with celebrity by running profiles of famous people. For example, television programs such as *Entertainment Tonight* devote all their programming to stories about entertainment and entertainers. Magazines such as *People* fill their pages with stories of the private lives of famous people. Even newspapers, newsmagazines, and television news frequently delve into the lives of well-known personalities. Despite the number of articles and programs, few provide more than a superficial glimpse at their subjects.

Lucent's People in the News series offers young readers a deeper look into the lives of today's newsmakers, the influences that have shaped them, and the impact they have had in their fields of endeavor and on other people's lives. The subjects of the series hail from many disciplines and walks of life. They include authors, musicians, athletes, political leaders, entertainers, entrepreneurs, and others who have made a mark on modern life and who, in many cases, will continue to do so for years to come.

These biographies are more than factual chronicles. Each book emphasizes the contributions, accomplishments, or deeds that have brought fame or notoriety to the individual and shows how that person has influenced modern life. Authors portray their subjects in a realistic, unsentimental light. For example, Bill Gates — the cofounder and chief executive officer of the software giant Microsoft—has been instrumental in making personal computers the most vital tool of the modern age. Few dispute his business savvy, his perseverance, or his technical expertise, yet critics say he is ruthless in his dealings with competitors and driven more by his desire to maintain Microsoft's dominance in the computer industry than by an interest in furthering technology.

In these books, young readers will encounter inspiring stories about real people who achieved success despite enormous obstacles. Oprah Winfrey—the most powerful, most watched, and wealthiest woman on television today—spent the first six years of her life in the care of her grandparents while her unwed mother sought work and a better life elsewhere. Her adolescence was colored by promiscuity, pregnancy at age fourteen, rape, and sexual abuse.

Each author documents and supports his or her work with an array of primary and secondary source quotations taken from diaries, letters, speeches, and interviews. All quotes are footnoted to show readers exactly how and where biographers derive their information and provide guidance for further research. The quotations enliven the text by giving readers eyewitness views of the life and accomplishments of each person covered in the People in the News series.

In addition, each book in the series includes photographs, annotated bibliographies, timelines, and comprehensive indexes. For both the casual reader and the student researcher, the People in the News series offers insight into the lives of today's newsmakers—people who shape the way we live, work, and play in the modern age.

A New Pope

On April 2, 2005, Pope John Paul II died. He had served as the spiritual leader for over 1 billion Catholics for twenty-six years. Cardinal Joseph Ratzinger, the pope's close friend and longtime associate, presided over his funeral. The cardinal spoke lovingly about the pope's struggles, triumphs, and dedication to the church. Then, his voice choked with emotion, he reassured the mourners that even though the pope was dead, he was still watching over them. "We can be sure that our beloved Pope is standing today at the windows of the Father's house, that he sees us and blesses us."[1] The cardinal's words consoled and touched the hearts of millions of mourners throughout the world.

A Controversial Figure

Prior to Pope John Paul II's death, Cardinal Ratzinger had worked side by side with the pope, serving as the prefect of the Congregation for the Doctrine of the Faith (CDF). It was his job to promote and defend the established principles and beliefs of the Catholic Church.

Every issue facing the church came across Cardinal Ratzinger's desk. His was the final word on issues such as abortion, birth control, homosexuality, and women in the priesthood and reflected the traditional values that both Ratzinger and the pope held.

Ruling on all these issues put Cardinal Ratzinger in a controversial role. Conservative Catholics praised Ratzinger for his rulings, while Catholics who wanted the church to modernize, criticized him severely, dubbing him the "Pope's Enforcer". And, the press often portrayed him as a stern, inflexible, and

Cardinal Joseph Ratzinger, serving as prefect of the Congregation for the Doctrine of the Faith (CDF), watches as Pope John Paul II signs a revised Code of Canon Law in 1983. Ratzinger's many years of influential work on the development and interpretation of church doctrine made him a leading candidate to replace Pope John Paul II when he died in 2005.

combative man. In reality, the cardinal was a scholarly person who disliked controversy, but, due to the nature of his job, was thrust into it.

Ratzinger's role at the pope's funeral showed the public his softer side. It helped them to understand that it was not the cardinal's personality that was fearsome and controversial but rather the job he held. Mourners, according to the Italian newspaper, *La Stampa*, were surprised "to discover behind the apparent aloofness of the scholar and the fame of the harsh guardian of the faith, a real father ... demanding but affectionate. It was well known that he was a brilliant scholar who had written dozens of books and could speak and/or read eight languages. What had been forgotten by many was that he was a kind and gentle pastor."[2] Not surprisingly, the cardinal was soon considered to be a possible successor to the pope.

Choosing a Pope

Sixteen days after the Pope John Paul II's death, on April 18, 2005, the Conclave of the Sacred College, 115 cardinals from fifty-two countries, met in the Sistine Chapel of the Vatican to choose the next pope. Since whoever they selected would direct the future of the Catholic Church, they had a lot to consider. They had to decide whether they wanted the new pope to continue in the path of John Paul II or if they wanted someone who would reform the church and take it in a new direction.

When the voting began, there were more than thirty candidates. The voting was done by secret ballot, so candidates did not know they were in the running until the votes were counted. To win, a candidate had to get at least two-thirds of the votes. Usually, it takes many days of repeated balloting before the field is narrowed down and a pope is chosen. But the conclave quickly united behind one candidate, Cardinal Joseph Ratzinger, the man they knew would continue Pope John Paul II's legacy. On the second day of balloting, he was selected to be the new pope. This was the second shortest conclave in papal history. According to Vatican expert, Otazio Petrosillo, "the cardinals chose continuity with serene certainty." The shortness of the conclave, he explained, gave "a strong sign of unity."[3]

Once the selection was made, Cardinal Ratzinger was asked whether he would accept the job. In truth, he dreamt of retiring to his home in Germany where he could live the quiet scholarly life that he so loved. "At a certain point [during the conclave] I prayed to God, 'Please don't do this to me,'" he recalls. "Evidently, this time he didn't listen to me."[4] Ratzinger's loyalty to the church, however, was stronger than his personal desires. Therefore, he accepted the papacy.

Ratzinger's decision made the assembled religious leaders very happy. German cardinal Walter Kasper commented: "I think he will be a pope of reconciliation and peace."[5]

A Healing Name

Next, Ratzinger had to choose his papal name. Because of the reputation he earned as prefect of the CDF, Ratzinger knew that his ascension to the papacy was apt to raise mixed emotion among Catholics, causing divisiveness between progressives and traditionalists. The new pope's goal was to bring unity to his flock. So, in an effort to bring people together, he chose the name Benedict XVI.

The last Pope Benedict, Benedict XV, served during World War I. In addition to the physical violence at that time, there were many different groups in the church arguing over philosophical issues. Pope Benedict XV was a peacemaker who worked tirelessly to end both the physical and philosophical battles that Catholics were engaged in. Pope Benedict XVI also wanted to bring peace and harmony to Catholics. The name Benedict symbolized this desire.

In addition, the name was a tribute to Saint Benedict, whose life was an inspiration to Ratzinger. St. Benedict founded monasteries that became centers of learning, charity, and hospitality for both religious leaders and the public. Pope Benedict XVI hoped to share these traditions with Catholics and non-Catholics, alike. In an article in the newspaper National Catholic Reporter, writer Richard P. McBrien explains: "The new pope in honoring both Benedict XV and St. Benedict of Nursia, may very well have forecast that his own papacy would be dedicated to healing and reconciliation, both inside and outside the church, and that he would try to be a wise and a flexible leader—a father to the entire Catholic community."[6]

A Humble Worker

Shortly after Pope Benedict XVI chose his papal name, he stepped out onto the central balcony of the Vatican to greet the crowds below. "Dear brothers and sisters," he said, "after the great Pope John Paul II, the Cardinals have elected me, a simple and humble laborer in the vineyard of the Lord. The fact that the Lord knows how to work and to act, even with inadequate instruments, comforts me, and above all I entrust myself to your prayers."[7]

Pope Benedict XVI greets crowds outside of St. Peter's Basilica in April 2005 after the announcement of his election by the College of Cardinals.

The pope waved to the cheering crowd, many of whom were impressed by his modesty, dignity, and serenity. Then, he went inside to begin his reign. Newspapers throughout the world speculated about whether the new pope would be able to unify Catholics, or if the controversy that had surrounded him in the past would stand in his way. The only thing that everyone could agree on, was that whatever Pope Benedict XVI did, it would have a lasting effect on the future of the Catholic Church and the world.

Chapter 1

Church and Family

Joseph Alois Ratzinger was born on April 16, 1927, in Marktl am Inn, a small town in Bavaria, a state located in southern Germany. He had a happy childhood that centered on his family and the Catholic Church.

Joseph was the third child of Joseph and Maria Ratzinger. His father was a police officer and his mother was a cook before she married. The family was not poor, but they did struggle financially.

The Ratzinger family lived in Marktl am Inn, a small Bavarian town in southern Germany. Joseph, the youngest of three children, was born in this home in April 1927.

The day of Joseph's birth was Holy Saturday, the day before Easter. It was also the day of his baptism, a religious ritual in which holy water is sprinkled on a person's head in order to purify him or her, and, in the case of infants, accept the baby into the Christian faith.

The holy water that was used to baptize Joseph was specially blessed for Easter, and the baby was the first person to be baptized with it. This, his parents believed, was a sign that the baby would have a special connection to the church. In his 1998 autobiography, the future pope explains: "To be the first person baptized with new water was seen as a significant act of Providence [fate]. I have always been filled with thanksgiving for having had my life immersed in this way in the Easter mystery, since this could only be a sign of blessing."[8]

The Center of Family Life

Much like other Bavarian families, the Ratzingers were a close-knit family whose life centered upon the church. The Ratzingers and their children, Joseph, Georg, and Maria, prayed together at mealtimes, sang hymns in the evenings, recited the rosary, and went to Mass every Sunday. "That was Joseph's upbringing," recalls Erika Kopp, Joseph's cousin. "There were lots of prayers. His father was a high-ranking policeman, and before he went on patrol, he would always make the sign of the cross."[9]

Such devotion was not unusual in Bavaria, a strongly Catholic region of Germany where community life typically centered upon the church. According to Ratzinger, village life was "structured in such a way that it enjoyed a firm symbiosis [interdependence] with the faith of the Church: birth and death, weddings and illnesses, sowing and harvest time—everything as encompassed by faith."[10] Indeed, no one in the village could imagine experiencing any important events in their lives without the church's involvement.

Not surprisingly, Joseph's life was defined from a young age by the church with its holidays, special ceremonies, prayers, and celebrations. He says, "The Church year gave the time its rhythm, and I experienced that with great gratitude and joy already as a child."[11]

The font at which Joseph was baptized into the Catholic faith on the day he was born in 1927 stands at St. Oswald Church in Marktl am Inn, Germany. Previously housed in a local museum, the font was restored and returned to the church upon Ratzinger's election as pope in 2005.

Happy Times and Big Ambitions

When Joseph was two years old, the family moved from Marktl am Inn to Tittmoning, a small town near the Austrian border. The family would move four times by the time Joseph was ten, but they never left Bavaria. Despite always being newcomers, Joseph and his brother and sister were rarely lonely. The three were good friends who enjoyed playing together.

In Tittmoning the family resided in the living quarters of the police station. It was a big, old building with steep staircases, crooked floors, and an attic. It was a perfect place for the children

Ratzinger's Parents

Ratzinger's parents, Maria and Joseph Ratzinger, met via a personal ad that Joseph placed in a newspaper. Joseph was a serious man who was strict with his children, but also loving and fair. He liked to go fishing with the children. After he retired, he spent many hours hiking in the woods of Traunstein with young Joseph. As they hiked, he often told the boy stories, which the future pope said brought them closer together.

Maria was a warm, kind person, who laughed easily. She was a wonderful cook and a gifted seamstress. She made young Joseph a collection of stuffed animals that he treasured. "Joseph's mother did a lot for him," recalls Joseph's cousin Erika Kopp. "She was very talented, and a hard worker. She made Joseph teddy bears and animals and rabbits, whatever you can think. She made them by hand. I was at Joseph's ordination on 20 June, 1951, and … he said to me, 'Erika, I've still got my animals.' Auntie was also a very good cook. She made these wonderful preserved walnuts and after our meal we were each given one."

Mark Lander and Richard Bernstein, "A Future Pope Is Recalled: A Lover of Cats and Mozart, Dazzled by the Church as a Boy," NYTimes.com, April 22, 2005, www.nytimes. com/2005/04/22/international/worldspecial2/22germany.html?ei=5088&en=deb8a c4c 18fa6d14&ex=1271822400&partner=rssnyt&emc=rss&pagewanted=all&position=.

to run, hide, and play. There was also plenty of room for the family's piano, which accompanied the Ratzingers wherever they moved. Music was an important part of the family's life. They would gather around the piano every evening and sing hymns, or listen as one of the parents played the music of Mozart. And, they often went to hear concerts in the nearby city of Salzburg. Not surprisingly, all of the children became accomplished pianists. In fact, Georg later became the musical director of the cathedral in Regensburg, Germany. And, Joseph, even as pope, continued to play the piano. Each evening he would have a glass of orange soda and play the piano for a half hour.

There was plenty to do outdoors too. The three children and their mother often hiked in the surrounding countryside where they looked for wild lettuce and gathered natural materials to use in their Christmas nativity scene, which grew in size each year.

Their involvement in the church also bound the family to whatever community they lived in. The children participated in church youth groups, and the two boys served as choir and alter boys. In fact, if Joseph had not been part of the church youth group, his life might have turned out differently. When he was five years old, the archbishop of Munich, Cardinal Michael Faulhaber, came to visit the local church. Joseph was part of a greeting committee made up of youth group members. The sight of the cardinal stepping out of his limousine, dressed in his rich robes and tall red hat, filled Joseph with awe. Right then, he decided that he, too, would be a cardinal someday. Georg Ratzinger recalls: "He came home and told our father that night, 'I want to be a cardinal.' It wasn't so much the car, since we weren't technically minded. It was the way the cardinal looked, his bearing, and the garments he was wearing that made such an impression on him."[12] It may be that this was the first step in Joseph's long road to becoming the pope.

Rising Trouble

Between their involvement in the local church and their large living quarters, the children were happy in Tittmoning. But life was not as pleasant for their parents. Losing World War I severely

*Nazi storm troopers march through Munich in 1934,
in the early days of the National Socialist Party's rule
in Germany. Adults and children alike were expected to
pledge allegiance to the party under threat of violence,
but many citizens, including the Ratzinger family, resisted.*

damaged the German economy and the morale of the German people. Bad conditions in Germany led to the rise of the National Socialist (Nazi) Party. Adolf Hitler, the leader of the Nazi Party promised to heal Germany, rid it of foreign influences, and turn it into a great world power. He wanted all Germans to join the party and give it their undivided loyalty. This meant transferring religious loyalty to loyalty to the party.

As the Nazis became more powerful, nonmembers were pressured to join the party. Those who refused were frequently victims of violence. Victims included a number of priests and nuns who were attacked on the streets and in their homes. Joseph's father was sickened by the violence. He viewed the Nazis as criminals and Nazism as a threat, both to his country and to the church. Although it was risky, he refused to join the party and spoke out against it. "He always expressed his indignation vigorously and always spoke freely to people whom he could trust. Above all, he never joined any organizations, even though he was a civil servant,"[13] recalls Ratzinger.

This stance made him enemies in Tittmoning. So, in December 1932 the family moved again, this time to the farming village of Aschau am Inn, at the foot of the alps. The family lived in a cozy little farmhouse surrounded by a large meadow and a small pond.

The children were quite happy in their new home, but the world was changing around them. Hitler became chancellor of Germany in 1933. On the day he took power, all the local schoolchildren were forced to march around the village waving Nazi flags. "I myself have no memory of that rainy day," Ratzinger says, "but my brother and sister have told me that the school had to perform a march through the village that, of course, soon turned into a tramp through the slush that could hardly have fired anyone's enthusiasm."[14]

A New Love

One of first actions Hitler's government took was to change what was taught in the schools. Until this point, religion was a key part of the curriculum in German schools. Hitler wanted German

A Look at Bavaria

Bavaria is the largest state in Germany. It is about 43,495 square miles (112,652 sq. km) in size, a little larger than the U.S. state of Virginia, and has more than 12 million people. Located in southern Germany, Bavaria borders Austria and the Czech Republic. Geographically, Bavaria is diverse. It contains snowcapped mountains, large rivers, rich farmland, old forests, and meadows. The natural beauty of the area attracts many hikers, mountain climbers, skiers, and tourists.

Bavaria is also one of the oldest states in Europe, having been established in the sixth century A.D. A number of ancient castles, which resemble those found in fairy tales, are found here. There are also many old churches and soaring cathedrals throughout Bavaria. Munich is the largest city in Bavaria.

children to learn about Nazism, not religion. Indoctrinating children in Nazism, Hitler believed, would make them loyal party members as adults. Consequently, government studies replaced religious studies in German schools.

Since religion was no longer emphasized in the village school the Ratzinger children attended, their parents took over the children's religious education. They gave their offspring specially illustrated missals, prayer books that contain all the prayers, hymns, and responses that comprise the Catholic Mass, which they read from daily.

Even at a young age, Joseph was quite studious. He loved to read and was thrilled with this new learning opportunity. He quickly advanced from his illustrated missal to more complex versions. Right away, he developed a fascination with the liturgy, the different prayers and rituals of the church. Its beauty and poetic nature touched the sensitive boy, who also wrote poetry. This fascination grew into a lifelong love of liturgy. He explains:

Every new step into the liturgy was a great event for me. Each new book I was given was something precious to me, and

The village of Marktl am Inn, the birthplace of Pope Benedict XVI, is typical of many small Bavarian towns nestled amid the mountains and rivers of southern Germany.

I could not dream of anything more beautiful. It was a riveting adventure to move by degrees into the mysterious world of the liturgy, which was being enacted before us, and for us there on the altar. It was becoming more and more clear to me that here I was encountering a reality that no one had simply thought up, a reality that no official authority or great individual created. This mysterious fabric of texts and actions had grown from the faith of the Church over the centuries. It bore the whole weight of history within itself and yet, at the same time, it was much more than a product of human history. … Naturally the child I then was did not grasp every aspect of this, but I started down the road of the liturgy, and this became a continuous process of growth for me.[15]

The Joy of Learning

Despite the close ties that bound the Ratzinger family to the church in Aschau am Inn, the family would move again. Joseph's father's hatred for the Nazis made it increasingly difficult for him to work for the government as a police officer. So, in 1937, at age sixty, he retired. The family bought an old farmhouse on the outskirts of Traunstein, a small city of eleven thousand people. The house had a leaky roof and lacked modern conveniences, such as running water. But, what it lacked in amenities it made up for in natural beauty. It looked out on the alps and was surrounded by fruit trees, meadows, and a thick pine forest. With its old barns and many rooms, it was a perfect playground for the children. They immediately fell in love with the place. It would be the family's final home, and Joseph's favorite. Years later he described the home in this way:

> Instead of tap water, there was a well, which was very picturesque. On one side of the house there was an oak forest interspersed with beeches, on the other side were the mountains … in terms of location it was heavenly. And in the old barns you could have the most marvelous dreams and play wonderful games. … It was a childhood dream. We felt altogether happy there even without comforts. For my father, who had to pay for the necessary repairs, for my mother, who carried water from the well, it was perhaps less fun. But we experienced it as a real paradise. … We didn't feel at all the lack of modern amenities, but experienced the adventure, freedom, and beauty of an old house with its inner warmth.[16]

Joseph was equally enchanted with his new school. The studious boy, who had an almost photographic memory, had already

The Ratzinger family sits for a family photo in 1938. Joseph is seated at left; brother Georg and sister Maria stand in the back, while parents Maria and Joseph are seated at right.

learned everything that the small village school in Aschau am Inn had to offer. In Traunstein he attended a gymnasium, a large public school, where he would study Greek and Latin. Although Joseph was the youngest child in the new school, he had no problem with these new and difficult subjects. In fact, he took pleasure in studying them. His knowledge of Latin and Greek helped him in his advanced studies later in life, especially since many ancient texts are written in these languages.

Seminary Life

After only two years in the gymnasium, the local priest, who was impressed with how seriously Joseph took his religious duties, urged the Ratzingers to send the boy to Saint Michael's Seminary in Traunstein, where Georg was already a student. Here students began preliminary studies toward the priesthood.

Unlike the gymnasium, the seminary was a boarding school, which charged tuition. The Ratzinger family could not afford to pay tuition for both boys. The future would have been much different for Joseph had his sister, Maria, not taken a job so she could help pay for Joseph's tuition. Such behavior was typical of the Ratzinger children who always tried to look after each other.

In the spring of 1939, Joseph entered the seminary. At first, he was not happy there. It was hard for him to adjust to living with sixty other boys in a highly structured environment. But his biggest challenge was participating in two hours of organized sports each day. Although his classmates did not mistreat him, he was the youngest boy in the seminary, and much smaller and weaker than the other boys. This put him at a disadvantage when it came

In 1939, when he was twelve years old, Joseph joined his brother Georg at St. Michael's Seminary in Traunstein, Germany, to begin his studies towards joining the priesthood.

to sports. Plus, he had never played organized sports before and had no talent for them. He recalls:

> I entered the seminary … with joy and great expectations. … However, I am one of those people who are not made for living in a boarding school. While at home I had lived and studied with great freedom, as I wished, and had built a childhood world of my own. Now I had to sit in a study hall with about sixty other boys, and this was such torture to me that studying, which had always come easy to me, now appeared almost impossible. But the greatest burden for me was … every day for two hours we had to participate in sports in the big playground at the seminary.[17]

Things became easier for Joseph in the fall of 1939 when the German government converted the building that housed the seminary into a military hospital to house soldiers injured in World War II. The seminary then moved to a former girl's school where there was no room for organized sports. Instead, the boys went hiking in the surrounding woods and fishing in the nearby streams. These were activities that Joseph loved. Little by little, he found himself making friends and adjusting to seminary life.

> We took group hikes in the afternoons, in the extensive woods of the surrounding area and played in the nearby mountain streams. We built dams, caught fish, and so forth. It was the kind of happy life boys should have. I came to terms, then, with being in the seminary and experiencing a wonderful time in my life. I had to learn how to fit into a group, how to come out of my solitary ways and start building a community with others by giving and receiving. For this experience I am very grateful because it was important to my subsequent life.[18]

Touched by War

Joseph spent two years living at the new school. Then in 1941, the German government commandeered the student's dormitory for, yet another, military hospital. Joseph and Georg were able to continue their studies while living at home, but not for long. In 1942, seventeen-year-old Georg was drafted into the German army. Although he did not support the government, he had no choice but to serve.

Joseph was allowed to continue his studies. But the war was drawing closer. Everyday, more seminarians were drafted and the news was filled with the deaths of boys that Joseph had known in the gymnasium. It would not be long until Joseph's scholarly existence would be disrupted again and the war would change his life.

Chapter 2

A Reluctant Warrior

Ratzinger's loyalty to and love for the church put him at odds with Hitler's government. He wanted as little to do with the Nazis as possible. But as the war lengthened, the German government forced younger and younger boys to take part. Outright defiance was punishable by death, as was the case of two famous student leaders in Munich who were executed by guillotine for distributing anti-Nazi literature. Even small acts of resistance could lead to imprisonment in a concentration camp. Yet, in his own quiet way, Joseph tried to resist when he could. But no matter how hard he tried, Joseph could not avoid the war. It was an experience that impacted him for the rest of his life.

Hitler Youth

When Joseph turned fourteen, he, along with all the other boys in his seminary class, was enrolled in the Hitler Youth movement. Enrollment was mandatory.

The organization prepared young men for Nazi Party membership. Members attended frequent meetings in which they marched, listened to speeches, and were indoctrinated in Nazism. Although Joseph risked punishment and the loss of the seminary tuition reduction he was now receiving, he refused to take part. This was a small, but dangerous act of resistance. According to Volker Dahm, the director of Nazi-era research for Munich's Institute of

Young German boys, members of the Hitler Youth, stand at attention in 1939. Joseph and the other boys in his seminary class, along with most other German adolescents, were forced to join the movement so that the government could indoctrinate them into the ways of the Nazi party.

Contemporary History, "some 80% to 90% of Germans joined the Hitler Youth, and refusing to sign up could mean being sent to a youth 'reeducation camp' akin to a concentration camp. You could try to avoid it but it was very, very difficult."[19]

Fortunately for Joseph, one of his teachers had the job of reporting attendance at the meetings. Because he liked Joseph, the teacher also took a risk and did not report the boy's absences. "When the compulsory Hitler Youth was introduced ... I was registered in the Hitler Youth. ... Thank goodness there was a very understanding mathematics professor. He himself was a Nazi, but an honest man, and said to me, 'Just go once to get the document so we have it…' When he saw that I simply didn't want to, he said, 'I understand, I'll take care of it' and so I was able to stay free of it,"[20] Ratzinger explains.

The Flak

Resistance would prove more difficult two years later. With the war going badly for Germany, the government started drafting sixteen-year-old boys.

In 1943 Joseph's entire seminary class was drafted into the Flak, an antiaircraft unit whose job was to protect German factories, roads, and railroads from aircraft fire. Joseph was trained to use electronic equipment to track and locate approaching aircraft. He gave the information to artillerymen who shot at the invaders. Joseph never fired a gun, a fact that he is still proud of.

His first assignment was protecting a Bavarian Motor Works (BMW) factory near Munich, which produced motors for trucks and airplanes used in the German war effort. Many of the workers in the factories were Jewish slave laborers taken from Dachau, a concentration camp. Like many other Germans, Joseph was not fully aware of the atrocities being committed against the Jews by the Nazi government. But the sight of the slave laborers touched the young man's heart. He would remember it years later when, as a cardinal, he openly criticized the church for not working harder to help the Jewish people during World War II. "His background gives him a special sensitivity in understanding the terror and evil of the Holocaust,"[21] explains Rabbi A. James Rudin of the American Jewish Committee.

Next, Joseph's unit was transferred to a railroad station near Innsbruck, Austria. Here his unit came under direct fire from allied aircraft. Several of the men were injured and one was killed. Even when his unit was not targeted specifically, since Allied planes were now dropping bombs on German cities on a daily basis, many of the cities his unit passed through were under attack. It was no wonder the teenager feared for his life. "The air

Joseph was only sixteen years old when he was drafted into the German army in 1943 to serve in the Flak, an anti-aircraft unit.

was more and more filled with smoke and the smell of fires. …
None of us could be sure that he would live to return home from
this inferno,"[22] he recalls. It was only Joseph's faith that helped
him cope.

No Rest

Joseph was discharged from the Flak on September 10, 1944, only
to be assigned to the labor service branch of the military. His unit
was sent to a camp on the border between Austria, Hungary, and
Slovakia, where he was forced to dig trenches aimed at blocking
Allied tanks that were now rolling toward Germany. It was back-
breaking physical labor, not at all suited to the bookish young
man. Making matters worse, the camp was located near a train

Hitler and the Jews

Jews were persecuted in Europe for centuries. When Hitler
came to power in 1933, six hundred thousand Jews lived
in Germany. Hitler used the Jews as scapegoats, blaming
Germany's economic and social problems on them.

The Nazis took away Jewish people's civil rights, citizenship,
jobs, and property in Germany, and later in the countries the
Nazis occupied. Then, in 1941, the Nazis came up with "the
final solution," which was a plan to totally wipe out all the
Jews in Europe.

Concentration camps with gas chambers disguised as show-
ers were created. Jews and other people that the Nazis considered "undesirable," including gypsies, handicapped individuals, homosexuals, and political dissidents, were rounded up and
transported to the camps, which the public believed were labor
camps. Indeed, some of the prisoners were used as slave labor,
but most were exterminated. By the close of World War II, the
Nazis had murdered between 5 and 6 million Jews.

station where the soldiers saw Hungarian Jews being shipped to Auschwitz, a concentration camp. Witnessing this took an emotional toll on Joseph. Author Michael Collins describes what was happening in this way: "He saw Hungarian Jews being moved like cattle in trains. Rumors circulated that they were being shipped to certain death. It was impossible not to be moved by the plight of these victims of Nazi arrogance. He was a young man trying desperately not to believe what was happening all about him."[23]

And, if all this was not hard enough to endure, Joseph's superior officers were fanatical Nazis, who bullied and tormented the young men in their command. In his biography Ratzinger recalls how these men tried to force their charges to join the weapons branch of the SS, a combat group that was later charged with war crimes. Despite being intimidated by the officers, Joseph resisted. He recalls:

> One night we were pulled out of bed and gathered together, half asleep in our exercise uniforms. An SS officer had each individual come forward, and, by taking advantage of our exhaustion and exposing each of us before the gathered group, attempted to make "voluntary" recruits for the weapons branch of the SS. A whole series of good-natured friends were in this way forced into this criminal group. With a few others, I had the good fortune of being able to say that I intended to become a Catholic priest. We were sent out with mockery and verbal abuse. But these insults tasted wonderful because they freed us from the threat of that deceitful "voluntary service" and all its consequences.[24]

Military Deserter

Hungary fell to the Allies in late October. In mid-November, the men in Ratzinger's unit were handed their civilian clothes and loaded into train cars, which would take them home. Although Ratzinger was elated at the thought of returning to Traunstein, the trip back was not easy for him. The train continuingly stopped due to air raids. The destruction he witnessed along the way was

In April 1945, Joseph deserted his unit and made his way to the Ratzinger home in Traunstein. To the family's relief, German officers who commandeered the home after Joseph's arrival did not force him back into service or punish him for his actions.

hard to bear. Vienna, Salzburg, and Munich were all in ruins. The cathedral in Salzburg, which he had visited with his family when they lived in Tittmoning, had been bombed and its elaborate dome destroyed.

When the train finally reached Traunstein, Ratzinger had to jump out of the moving vehicle. Coming to a stop would have made it an easy target for Allied aircraft in the area. Seeing his hometown again filled Ratzinger with such joy that flinging himself out of a moving train was of no concern to the unathletic young man. "It was," he remembers, "an idyllically beautiful fall day. There was a bit of hoarfrost on the trees and the mountains glowed in the afternoon sun. Seldom have I ever experienced the beauty of my homeland as on this return from a world disfigured by ideology [belief in a philosophy] and hatred."[25]

Ratzinger spent three weeks in his family home; then he received orders to report to an infantry unit with barracks in Traunstein. Although the Allies had invaded Germany and were moving closer and closer to Traunstein, Ratzinger's unit did not see action. Mainly, they were forced to march around the city singing war songs. This was supposed to convince the civilian population that the war was going well for Germany. In reality, it was only a matter of time before Germany surrendered. But Ratzinger could not wait any longer. He had enough of war and military life.

So, in another act of resistance, in April 1945 he deserted his unit and headed for the Ratzinger cottage. Later, Ratzinger's critics would say that this was not a significant act, since the war was almost over and many other German soldiers were deserting. However, since deserters faced execution, leaving his unit was a serious step. Johannes Tuchel, the director of the German Resistance Memorial in Berlin, puts it this way:

> The color of resistance is not black or white, it's a scale of grey. It was not a single decision, not a single choice—you didn't just say one day I resist. Everyday you had to decide if you were going to go with the Nazi system or step aside. … There was always a choice. You have to go into the Hitler Youth, but then it is your decision if you are going to be an active member. You have to go into the labor service, but it's

your decision if you're very active. You had no choice to go into the army, but it is your decision how long you stay."[26]

In an effort to avoid discovery, Ratzinger took the back roads home. This did not prevent him from encountering two soldiers guarding a railroad underpass. The meeting terrified Ratzinger who expected the soldiers to shoot him on sight. However, due to a recent accident, Ratzinger's arm was in a sling. Thinking the boy was wounded in action, the soldiers let him pass.

Even when he reached his home, Ratzinger was not safe. He had barely arrived, when a German air force officer demanded a bed in the Ratzinger household. He could have turned Ratzinger in, but, possibly because he was a fellow Catholic, or because he realized the war was almost over, he did not report Ratzinger's presence. Shortly thereafter, two SS officers commandeered the house for their headquarters. The family suspected that these

Hitler and the Church

In 1933 Adolf Hitler and Pope Pius XI signed a document known as a concordant. In it, the pope promised that the Catholic Church would not interfere in German politics or domestic policy. In exchange, Hitler promised to protect the church and allow Catholics to worship in peace. Although the pope did not fully trust Hitler, he felt that signing the agreement was the best way to protect Catholics under Nazi rule.

Hitler did not honor his promise. One of Hitler's goals was the destruction of Christianity and the Catholic Church in particular. The Nazis closed down Catholic schools, youth groups, newspapers, and labor organizations. They falsely accused many priests and nuns of scandalous crimes in an effort to make the church look bad. And, more than seven hundred dissenting priests and an unknown number of nuns were killed in Nazi concentration camps. In 1937 the pope denounced the Nazis.

were the same men responsible for hanging sixty-two deserters in the nearby woods. Naturally, finding a boy of military age in the Ratzinger's house aroused the officers' suspicions. However, with the American army rapidly approaching, the SS officers cut short their stay, leaving Ratzinger unharmed. It was, to his mind, as if an angel had been watching over him. He explains:

> In the course of the next few days there lodged with us, first, a sergeant-major of the air force, an agreeable Catholic from Berlin, who following a strange logic we could not understand, still believed in the victory of the "German Reich". My father who argued extensively with him on this matter, was finally able to win him over to our side. Then, two SS men were given shelter in our house, which made the situation doubly dangerous. They could not fail to see that I was of military age, and so they began to make inquiries about my status. It was a known fact that a number of soldiers who had left their units had already been hanged from trees by SS men. Besides, my father could not help voicing all his ire [anger] against Hitler to their faces, which as a rule should have had deadly consequences for him. But a special angel seemed to be guarding us, and the two disappeared the next day without having caused any mischief.[27]

Prisoner of War

A few days after the SS officers departed, the American army arrived in Traunstein. Ratzinger, along with a steadily growing group of young men, was taken by the Americans as a prisoner of war (POW). The prisoners were forced to march for three days to an airport in Bad Aibling, Germany. From there, they were transferred to open farmland, surrounded by barbed wire fences, near the city of Ulm.

By the time the prisoners reached Ulm, their numbers topped fifty thousand. Conditions in the POW camp were harsh. The Americans did not have tents or other shelter for the prisoners, who were forced to sleep out in the rain. Nor, was there enough food. Daily rations consisted of a ladleful of soup and a little piece

Pope Pius XI was seeking protection for the Catholic Church when he signed a concordant with German chancellor Adolf Hitler in 1933. Four years later, however, as Hitler repeatedly and violently violated the agreement, the pope issued an encyclical denouncing Nazism.

of bread. But daily religious services conducted by fellow prisoners of war made life in the camp more bearable for Ratzinger.

The POWs had no clocks, calendars, or newspapers. They had trouble keeping track of the date and did not know what was going on in the world. Rumors abounded. The men had no idea what was going to happen to them, or if Germany had surrendered. There was talk that the men would be put on trial for war crimes or sent off to fight the Russians, whose wartime alliance with Germany's enemies was quickly unraveling. Ratzinger explains:

> On May 8 the Americans, who were always firing a few shots in the air, suddenly started shooting like mad—it was a real fireworks show. Then the rumor spread that the war was over, that Germany had surrendered. At that point we breathed a sigh of relief. … However, the rumor immediately spread that we shouldn't rejoice too soon because the Americans would now start fighting against the Russians. We would be armed again and sent against the Russians. However, I couldn't imagine that the Alliance had come to pieces so quickly and didn't believe the report. I was simply happy the war was over and only hoped this business wouldn't last too long.[28]

Finally Free

Just as Ratzinger hoped, the Americans started releasing the prisoners. On June 14, 1945, Ratzinger was interrogated and released. He was transported to Munich, then had to make his way to Traunstein, a distance of 75 miles (121km). He teamed up with another boy and began walking toward his home. The boys, who had neither money nor rations, expected the trip would take three days. They planned to sleep in the fields and beg food from sympathetic farming families. But luck smiled upon them. A milk truck heading to Traunstein came along. Although the boys were too shy to signal it to stop, the driver took pity on them and offered them a ride. As a result, Ratzinger arrived in Traunstein that same day.

As he stood in the town square, he heard singing coming from the church. Although he suspected his family was inside, Ratzinger did not want to interrupt the services, so he went straight home. He walked into the house, surprising his father, who had not attended services that day. The older man was astonished to see him and the two had a joyous reunion. The emotional scene was repeated a little while later when Ratzinger's mother and sister arrived home from church.

As the days passed, there was only one thing marring the little family's happiness. No one had heard from Georg since early April. He had been posted to Italy where the bombing and fighting had been heavy. The family feared he was dead or seriously wounded.

In late July, however, Georg returned home. He had been held in an Allied prisoner of war camp near Naples, Italy. When he walked through the door, the Ratzinger's happiness was complete. They were finally reunited and free of Nazi bondage. Full of joy and thanksgiving, the family celebrated Georg's return by gathering around the piano and singing a hymn of thankfulness.

The following months were especially happy for Ratzinger. They were, according to him, "full of a sense of newly won freedom, something we were only now learning to really treasure. ... Many had fallen in the war, and we who returned home were all the more grateful for the gift of life and for the hope that again rose high above all the destruction."[29]

Ratzinger felt blessed that he and his family had survived the war. Throughout his ordeal, his religion gave him strength and helped him cope with all that was going on around him. He resolved to resume his studies and become a priest. In so doing, he hoped to put the terrible ordeal behind him. But he would never forget the atrocities that loyalty to Nazism caused. He vowed to always put the church first no matter the cost.

Chapter 3

Priest and Scholar

Putting the war behind him, Ratzinger began many happy years of academic life. But student uprisings in the 1960s shook his world. Once again he felt that loyalty to an ideology was a threat to the church. So, he resisted.

A New Start

Shortly before Christmas 1945, Ratzinger and Georg entered the seminary in Freising, a small city near Munich. The brothers were among 120 students beginning the six years of study that would qualify them for the priesthood.

From the start, Ratzinger was an enthusiastic student who read everything he could get his hands on. He was often seen sitting in a corner reading a novel or an important work of philosophy or religion. But Ratzinger did not have as much time to read as he may have liked, since the seminarians were kept very busy. Author Greg Watts describes seminary life:

> From the moment Joseph took his seat in the classroom for his first lecture, he had very little free time. The daily timetable in seminaries in Europe in the 1940s was ruled by bells and was highly structured. Studies included Latin, which Joseph enjoyed, as he felt it opened up the thinking of civilizations of the ancient world, New Testament Greek, and Old Testament Hebrew. The heart of the seminary was the chapel, where each day the students attended Mass, the Angelus at midday, and sang Lauds [dawn prayers], Vespers

A Respected Writer

For as long as he can remember, Pope Benedict XVI has loved to write. As a child, he wrote poetry. As an adult, he has written more than forty books on religion and religious history. Many of his books have been best sellers that have been translated into dozens of languages and reprinted multiple times. Theology students throughout the world use his books for reference. Because his writing is clear and easy to read, his books are also popular with ordinary people.

He is also the author of hundreds of articles and essays. During Vatican II, he wrote articles for German publications reporting on what was happening in Rome. At the University of Regensburg, he helped start *Communio*, a well-respected Catholic journal that has an international circulation and as of 2008 was published in seventeen languages. Until he became pope, Ratzinger was a frequent contributor to the journal.

In addition to his religious writings, Ratzinger has also written about music, art, and architecture.

[evening prayers], and Compline [night prayers]. ... They would not only have been expected to spend regular periods in meditation, but also take responsibility for keeping the corridors and rooms clean and the gardens tidy. The *magnum silencium* [rule of silence] was imposed each night. ... The strict rules and regulations were intended to form a student's character, Joseph would have been told. ... Students were taught not to be concerned with their personal comfort, but rather with their soul. Each one had to see to his own soul, if he was to save those of others. The key to holiness was to cultivate a deep life of prayer, which would help them grow into men of equally deep faith.[30]

The time flew by for Ratzinger. When his two years in Freising were over, he entered the University of Munich for his final four years of seminary study. Because much of the university had been

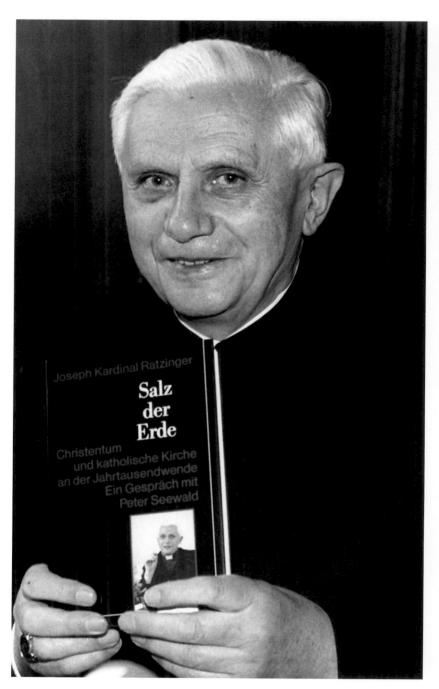

Cardinal Ratzinger holds a copy of Salt of the Earth, *one of the more than 40 books he has written on religious topics.*

destroyed during the war, the seminarians were housed in an old hunting lodge. The building was small and dilapidated, but it was located adjacent to a beautiful old castle and a wooded park with cheerful gardens, where Ratzinger often went to think, read, and study. With more books at his disposal, Ratzinger added books on physics, mathematics, and world religions to his reading list. His main course of study was theology, or religious studies. The lectures were held in the park's greenhouse, which was bitter cold in winter and overly hot in summer. But the curriculum was so absorbing that Ratzinger did not mind. He explains, "I was fascinated by academic theology. I found it wonderful to enter into the great world of the history of faith; broad horizons of thought and faith opened up before me."[31]

The Competition

Ratzinger's four years at the University of Munich were one of the happiest periods in his life. He easily passed his final exam in the summer of 1950. He was expected to spend the next few months preparing for his ordination into the priesthood. This involved hours of training in the practical aspects of being a priest, such as learning to write sermons and memorizing the detailed movements and prayers for the Mass.

During this time, an unexpected opportunity came his way. He was asked to enter an essay contest, which, if he won, would help him to earn a doctoral degree. Ratzinger dreamed of earning an advanced degree and going on to teach theology in a university. Many priests at the time served as professors in German universities. To hold such a position was a perfect match for the bookish Ratzinger, who loved learning and sharing his knowledge with others. Moreover, he would have plenty of time to write, which he enjoyed tremendously and had a real talent for. "Pretty early on, already in elementary school, a desire to teach awoke in me. I'm grateful that this desire fit so well with the idea of the priesthood,"[32] he explains.

The essay, which was book length, was on the teachings of Saint Augustine. The saint believed that God was a part of every person and that individuals could come to know themselves and God better through prayer. It was a philosophy that Ratzinger wholeheartedly embraced. Indeed, Saint Augustine was one of the young man's heroes.

Although it was quite a challenge, Ratzinger managed to write the essay and practice for his ordination at the same time. In fact, Ratzinger won first prize in the contest.

A Priest

Ratzinger now dedicated himself to preparing for his ordination. The happy day occurred on June 29, 1951, at the cathedral in Freising. Cardinal Michael Faulhaber, the same man who had inspired Ratzinger when he was a little boy, ordained forty young men, including Ratzinger and Georg that day. It was one of the high points of Ratzinger's life, filling him with joy and wonder. He recalls: "At the moment when the elderly archbishop laid his hands on me, a little bird—perhaps a lark—flew up from the high altar in the cathedral and trilled a little joyful song. And I could not help but see in this a reassurance from on high, as if I heard the words 'this is good, you are on the right way.'"[33]

Ratzinger was appointed assistant pastor at the Church of Precious Blood in Munich, where on a typical day, he heard confessions for one to four hours; celebrated at least one mass; visited the sick; presided over funerals, weddings, and baptisms; supervised youth groups; and gave religious instructions to children. It was this last task, which he most enjoyed. According to Ratzinger,

I had to teach sixteen hours of religious education a week. Not only that, I had to do that in six different grades, from the second to the eighth. That's a hefty bundle of work, especially when you're just beginning. In terms of the amount of time, that was my main occupation, which I came to love, because I very quickly formed a good relationship with the children. For me, it was interesting to step outside of the intellectual sphere for a change and to learn to talk with children. It was quite a wonderful thing to translate the

The Ratzinger family gathers to celebrate Georg and Joseph's ordination into the priesthood in July 1951. From left are sister Maria, Georg, mother Maria, brother Joseph, and father Joseph.

whole world of abstract concepts in such a way that it also said something to a child.

Every Sunday I had three homilies [sermons], one children's homily and two for adults. To my amazement, the children's Mass was the best attended of all, because now suddenly the adults started coming too. I was the only curate, and in addition to that I also took care of the whole youth ministry alone every evening. Every week I had baptisms and also a lot of burials ... where I rode right through Munich on my bicycle.[34]

Return to Academic Life

Ratzinger spent only one year at the Church of Precious Blood. In October 1952 he was reassigned to the seminary in Freising, where he instructed seminarians. While there, he prepared for and took a grueling test, which qualified him for his doctorate degree in July 1953. Shortly thereafter, he began work toward a

Father Ratzinger celebrates an outdoor Mass in the mountains outside of Munich in 1952.

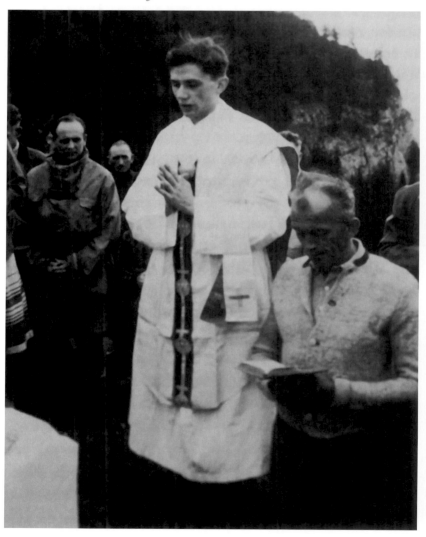

second degree known as a habilitation, which would qualify him to be a full professor of theology at a German university. To earn this degree, he had to write a second book-length essay. This one dealt with the teachings of Saint Bonaventure. With a full teaching schedule to contend with, preparing the essay was a difficult task. Nevertheless, Ratzinger managed to do so. Now, his future was in the hands of two theology professors who would either accept or reject the work.

One professor liked Ratzinger's paper. The other rejected it. He said it was poorly written and overlooked the work of other scholars who had researched the subject. Ratzinger did not receive his habilitation. What made matters worse was that Ratzinger's parents were getting old and could no longer live alone. So, they were living with Ratzinger. Without his habilitation, the young priest would probably be reassigned to a distant parish. This meant that his parents, who were barely getting use to living in Freising, would have to move again. Ratzinger's only hope was to rewrite the essay. This type of project generally took years to complete; but with the help of his sister, who typed the work, Ratzinger managed to rewrite the paper in just two weeks. Such a feat was unheard of. What made it all the more astounding was that the new document was highly praised and Ratzinger, therefore, was awarded his advanced degree.

A Popular Professor

Word of Ratzinger's accomplishment spread through the academic world. Almost every German university wanted the scholarly priest on their faculty. But Ratzinger did not want to uproot his parents. Therefore, even though it was his dream to be a part of a large important university where he could exchange ideas with the greatest scholars of the time, he turned down every offer. Instead he took a position at the University of Munich, which was not as prestigious as some of the other offers, but it would allow him to remain in Freising with his parents.

Circumstances changed in 1959 when Georg Ratzinger became the choir director at the seminary in Traunstein and the elder

Father Ratzinger lectures at a seminary in Freising, Germany, in 1955. His skill as a lecturer and his scholarly work gained him great respect in the academic world.

Ratzingers, who missed their hometown, decided to live with him. With his parents taken care of, Ratzinger became a professor of theology at the University of Bonn, a highly respected university with a world-famous theology faculty.

Ratzinger loved his life in Bonn. He took great pleasure in his work and in the busy city he now called home. He visited museums, attended concerts, and made friends with scholars of diverse backgrounds and interests. According to author Michael

Collins, "the intellectual stimulation was all that he had hoped for. … The young Ratzinger was fascinated to meet his colleagues who debated issues which he had never heard addressed seriously during his training."[35] The experience opened Ratzinger's mind to new ideas and made him more worldly.

Ratzinger's happiness, however, was marred by the death of his father on August 28, 1958. The older man had suffered a stroke a few days earlier, and his whole family was at his bedside when he died. It was a great loss to Ratzinger, but his faith helped him to cope. "I sensed the world was emptier for me and that a portion of my home had been transferred to the other world,"[36] Ratzinger recalls.

Called to Rome

Ratzinger's work in Bonn was earning him a reputation as a brilliant scholar. So, when Pope John XXIII called for the Second Vatican Council, commonly known as Vatican II, Cardinal Frings of Cologne asked Ratzinger to accompany him to Rome and serve as his theological adviser. The council consisted of more than twenty-six hundred bishops and cardinals who would meet every fall from 1962 to 1965. Their job was to discuss and decide how the church could update the faith in order to meet the challenges of the modern world. The First Vatican Council had been held in 1869. Before that, a council took place in the 1500s. Since the last such council had taken place so long ago, the group had a lot to do. As Cardinal Fring's theological adviser, Ratzinger was charged with studying how the church had responded to various issues in the past.

Ratzinger started preparing for his work on the council in 1960, dividing his time between his teaching duties and studying church history. His schedule became even more hectic once the council commenced. The constant travel and heavy workload, which included writing all the cardinal's speeches, took a toll on Ratzinger, as did the death of his mother in 1963.

But Ratzinger's hard work paid off. It influenced the passage of many of the reforms that Vatican II established, including

Over 2,600 church leaders gather in St. Peter's Basilica in December 1965 for the final session of the Second Vatican Council. Father Ratzinger attended the council as an adviser to Cardinal Frings of Cologne, Germany.

promoting unity with other Christian religions and modernizing the Congregation for the Doctrine of the Faith. Father Ratzinger's work on Vatican II earned him an international reputation as a gifted theologian. According to well-known Catholic author and journalist, Vittorio Messori, "he won the esteem ... of those who saw in this historic gathering a singular, unique opportunity to adapt ... to the times."[37]

Controversial Changes

For the most part, Ratzinger was pleased with the changes Vatican II had made. Although he was not comfortable with those reforms that affected traditional rites and rituals, such as changing the Mass from Latin to the local language of the congregation. He worried that it would detract from the beauty and mystery of the traditional Mass.

Ratzinger was not alone in his worries. The changes that Vatican II brought about were controversial. Some of the members of the council felt that Vatican II had not gone far enough and more sweeping reforms were needed. Others feared that the reforms would tear down the foundation the church was built upon. And, without proper guidance, some theologians would take the changes too far. Author Peter Hebblethwaite put it this way: "If changes were possible in the sphere of liturgy [prayers and rituals] which for centuries had remained invariable, then change would be possible in any area of religious life; and that thought led to another, which did not long remain unexpressed: where will it all end?"[38]

A Celebrity

Ratzinger, who did not like controversy or confrontation, seemed to be caught in the middle. He was, therefore, happy when the council finally ended and he could return to his peaceful academic life. In 1966 he took a position at the University of Tubingen. It was a large, prestigious university located close to Bavaria, which made it possible for him to see his brother and sister more frequently.

Students and workers demonstrate in demand of government reforms in Paris in 1968, one of many examples of the increased social and political activism among young people in Europe and America in the 1960s.

The reputation that Ratzinger had earned through his work on Vatican II made him a celebrity at Tubingen, and his talent as a teacher made him wildly popular. His seminars were so packed that students had to take an entrance exam to attend and, even then, there was standing room only. In an article by Gianni Valente, published in *30 Days*, an international journal, the author and Helmut Moll, one of Father Ratzinger's former students, explain why Ratzinger was so popular. According to Valente, "his enthusiasm and the unmistakable shape of his lectures—substantial theology … luminous and nimble language … frank response to all the questions of those confused times—kindled an unexpected response in the hearts of many students of theology. …

The 1960s

Many historians describe the 1960s as a period of social revolution. Throughout the world, young people were trying to change society and governments, while experimenting with alternative lifestyles. Many were involved in counterculture activities, such as communal living, using psychedelic drugs, and antigovernment protests.

In the United States antiwar protests against the country's involvement in the Vietnam War caused divisiveness among Americans. At the same time, the civil rights movement was changing society. Through peaceful protest, it helped gain equal rights for African Americans. The feminist movement, which was concerned with gaining equality for women, was also beginning.

In Europe a student uprising in France, aimed at supporting striking workers, almost crippled the nation. Throughout Western Europe, more and more young people were adopting communism or socialism as a political philosophy. Student protests, which shut down universities, became more and more common.

A crowd of more than four hundred students immediately packed his lectures. Too many also attended his seminars, so they had to be thinned out by a Greek and Latin entry exam." Helmut Moll recalls: "There was no comparison between Ratzinger and the others. The lectures that I heard in Bonn from [other] professors … appeared arid and cold, a list of precise … definitions and that was it. When I listened in Tubingen to Ratzinger speaking … it seemed at times that his words had the accent of prayers."[39]

And, because Ratzinger believed that religion should be shared with everyone, he developed a series of early morning public lectures. Students, townspeople, priests, Catholics, and non-Catholics flocked to these lectures. From them Ratzinger wrote a book called *Introduction to Christianity*, which became an international best seller.

Turbulent Years

At first, Ratzinger was happy in Tubingen. But by 1968, the controversy that surrounded Vatican II found its way to the university and the campus was rocked by student rebellion. Many Tubingen students wanted to make even more radical changes to the church. Because of his work on Vatican II, the students expected Ratzinger to support them. But he did not. Nor, did he approve of the growing popularity of Marxism among many of the students. It is the ideology that led to the rise of communism. Ratzinger saw in it the same dangers that he had seen in Nazism.

Although other professors tried to ignore the students or pretended to go along with them, Ratzinger tried to reason with them. This made them angry. Father Ratzinger soon became the object of student protests. His classes were disrupted, he was verbally abused, and the church and his beliefs were mocked. Max Seckler, then the dean of the Catholic theological faculty at Tubingen recalls: "The university was in chaos. It was horrible. The students kept professors from talking. They were verbally abusive, very primitive, and aggressive, and this aggression was especially directed against Ratzinger."[40]

A Peaceful Place

The students' behavior shocked and sickened Ratzinger. In 1969 he took a position at the University of Regensburg, where the student body was more conservative. And, he would be living in the same city as his brother and sister. Ratzinger's years at the University of Regensburg were among his happiest. Although he hoped to stay there for the rest of his life, his dedication to the church would lead him down a different path.

Chapter 4

Protector of the Faith

Ratzinger's plan to spend his life teaching, writing, and studying at the University of Regensburg hit a snag when the church needed him for other things. Although he did not want to leave the little house he shared with his sister or his peaceful academic life, he heeded the call. As he rose up in the church hierarchy, he became a controversial figure. Yet, at heart, he remained a gentle and quiet scholar.

Archbishop and Cardinal

In 1976 the archbishop of Munich and Freising died. Pope Paul VI, who succeeded Pope John XXIII, knew of Ratzinger's work on Vatican II. The pope respected Ratzinger's work and selected him to fill the position. Being archbishop of Munich and Freising involved supervising and guiding all the bishops and priests in the diocese, which consisted of more than 750 parishes led by about eight hundred priests.

Ratzinger was fifty years old at the time, and he had never served as a bishop. Being appointed an archbishop without first being a bishop, and, at such a young age, was a great honor. Nevertheless, Ratzinger was not eager to accept the appointment. His calling, he felt, was to teach, write, and study.

Father Ratzinger greets some of his young followers in May 1977 after being nominated by Pope Paul VI to serve as archbishop of Munich and Freising. One month later, he was elevated to cardinal.

Ratzinger talked to Georg and to his own priest about the decision before him. When they both told him that it was his duty to accept the position, he reluctantly did so. He said:

> I had, of course, very great doubts at first about whether I should or ought to accept the appointment. ... I felt that, in principle, I was called from the beginning to teach and believed that at this period of my life—I was fifty years old—I had found my own theological vision. ... I then took counsel

and was told that in an extraordinary situation such as we live in today, it is also necessary to accept things that don't seem to be in the direction of one's life from the beginning.[41]

In May 1977 Ratzinger was ordained at the Cathedral of Our Lady in Munich. The cathedral, which had been damaged in World War II, was no longer as grand as it had been. But the many flowers and decorations that had been placed throughout the cathedral for the ceremony added color and warmth to the atmosphere, and filled Ratzinger with joy. The ceremony was followed by a prayer session in the center of the city. Hundreds of spectators, many of whom knew little about Ratzinger, attended the prayer session. They all welcomed him as their new bishop. According to Ratzinger, it was a very moving experience:

The encounter with so many people who were welcoming this unknown person with a heartfelt warmth and joy that could not possibly have had to do with me personally but that once again showed me what a sacrament [a religious rite that brings joy to those participating in it] is: I was being greeted as bishop, as bearer of the Mystery of Christ, even if the majority were not explicitly [clearly] conscious of this. The joy of the day was something really different from the approval of a particular person, whose qualifications still had to be demonstrated. It was a joy over the fact that the office, this service, was again present in a person who does not act and live for himself but for Him [God] and therefore for all.[42]

Only a month later, Pope Paul VI raised Ratzinger up again and made him a cardinal. Cardinal Ratzinger endeared himself to the people in his diocese by visiting the many local churches where he personally conducted services.

A Strong Connection

Ratzinger had been a cardinal for a little more than a year when Pope Paul VI died in August 1978. One of a cardinal's most important duties is participating in the Conclave of the Sacred College

Cardinal Karol Wojtyla of Krakow, Poland, who later became Pope John Paul II, befriended Cardinal Ratzinger when the two men met in 1978 at the Conclave of the Sacred College of Cardinals following the death of Pope Paul VI.

of Cardinals, which selects a new pope. Ratzinger went to Rome to take part in the election. At the conclave he met Cardinal Karol Wojtyla of Krakow, Poland. The two men immediately connected. Although one was German and the other Polish, they shared a common bond. Both men's lives had been negatively affected by ideologies that attempted to take the place of religion—Nazism in Ratzinger's case and communism in Wojtyla's. Their experiences made them want to protect the church at all costs. In addition, both men were satisfied with the changes Vatican II made and saw no need for more drastic reforms. Plus, the two cardinals were scholars who were unafraid to speak their minds. And, they shared a similar sense of humor and an interest in religious history. They became fast friends. Ratzinger describes what attracted him to the Polish cardinal who would become Pope John Paul II in the future:

> The first thing that won my sympathy was his uncomplicated human frankness and openness, as well as the cordiality that he radiated. There was his humor. ... Here was a person ... who was really a man of God and, what is more, a completely original person who had a long intellectual and personal history behind him. ... He lived through the whole drama of German occupation, of the Russian occupation, [of Poland] and of the Communist regime. He blazed his own intellectual trail. He studied German philosophy intensively; he entered deeply into the whole intellectual history of Europe. ... This intellectual wealth, as well as his enjoyment of dialogue and exchange, these were all things that immediately made him likeable to me.[43]

A Brief Reign

Cardinal Albino Luciani of Venice was elected the new pope. He took the papal name John Paul. After only thirty-three days in office, Pope John Paul suddenly died. Ratzinger returned to Rome to take part in the election of John Paul's successor.

The College of Cardinals had a big decision to make. Two popes had died in the same year. Both had been old men. Many of the cardinals thought it would be wise to elect a younger man this time. Ratzinger's friend Cardinal Wojtyla of Krakow was fifty-eight years old. Ratzinger thought Wojtyla would make a good pope and actively campaigned for him. In what was a radical change of course, Wojtyla was elected pope. He was the youngest pope to be elected in a century, the first Polish pope, and the first non-Italian to fill the position in over four hundred years.

The dome of St. Peter's Basilica dominates a view of the Vatican, which includes many other buildings of historical and religious significance.

The Vatican

The Vatican is a unique place. With a population of about nine hundred people and an area of 0.17 square miles (0.44 sq. km), it is the smallest independent state in the world. Located within the city of Rome, the Vatican is surrounded by walls and ruled over by the pope. Among the many buildings within its 108 acres (44ha) is the Apostolic Palace, where the pope and cardinals, who are members of the nine congregations that serve the pope, live. There are also a number of museums, which contain masterpieces of art dating back thousands of years.

The Vatican is also the home of one of the oldest astronomical observatories in existence. It was built in 1578. A more recent addition to the Vatican is the film library, which contains historical film on different popes and religious events. There is also a huge library that contains a multitude of books and manuscripts. In addition, there is a secret archive where confidential documents, dating back to 1660, are stored.

The buildings are surrounded by beautiful gardens that were first planted in 1297. A colony of parrots lives in the trees. Throughout history, popes have strolled and meditated here.

From the start, the new pope wanted Cardinal Ratzinger to join him in Rome. There were many jobs Ratzinger could fill. But Ratzinger had not been a cardinal long and felt his duty was to the people of Munich. Pope John Paul II understood and said he would wait, but not for long.

Prefect of the Congregation for the Doctrine of the Faith

Ratzinger remained in contact with his friend, Pope John Paul II. In 1980 the pope honored Ratzinger by visiting Munich. Once again, he requested that Ratzinger come to Rome.

He wanted Ratzinger to become the new head, or prefect, for the Congregation for the Doctrine of the Faith (CDF). He trusted that the German cardinal would uphold the traditional values the two men shared. Ratzinger preferred to remain in Munich. He knew that accepting the appointment would reduce what little time he currently had to write and study. But, once again, dedication to the church made him put aside his personal desires and accept the position. He explains:

> For me, becoming Prefect of the Congregation for the Faith, the cost was that I couldn't do full time what I had envisaged

Cardinal Ratzinger celebrates his farewell to Munich in February 1982 after accepting Pope John Paul II's request for him to serve as the prefect of the Congregation for the Doctrine of the Faith at the Vatican.

for myself. … I had to descend to the little and various things pertaining to factual conflicts and events. I had to leave aside a great part of what would interest me and simply serve and to accept that as my task. And I had to free myself from the idea that I absolutely have to write or read this or that. I had to acknowledge that my task is here.[44]

In November 1981 Cardinal Ratzinger became the prefect of the CDF. According to church law, the primary role of the Congregation, "is to promote and safeguard the doctrine on the faith and morals throughout the Catholic world: for this reason everything which in any way touches such matter falls within its competence."[45] As prefect, Ratzinger's many duties included fostering knowledge of the faith, disciplining clergymen whose teachings the congregation found to be unacceptable, examining and correcting the writings of church leaders to make sure they did not oppose church teachings, speaking out against dangerous practices and doctrines, examining offenses against the faith, and punishing those who defied church law.

In the past, the prefect of the CDF conducted witch trials and acted as the grand inquisitor during the Spanish inquisition, meting out punishments that included death. Primarily due to Ratzinger's work on Vatican II, the prefect of the CDF could no longer carry out severe punishments. Instead, he could issue a reprimand or, in severe cases, excommunicate the offender, which means officially excluding the offender from taking part in church rituals. However, because of the power the prefect wielded in the past, many people consider him to be a rigid and frightening figure. So, Ratzinger knew that taking the position would not make him popular.

Hot Issues

Ratzinger also knew that the job of prefect of the CDF would be difficult. It put him in the center of many controversial issues. Ratzinger's rulings on these issues do not reflect his personal opinion, but rather are based on his interpretation of the teachings of the church. And, Ratzinger did not make any decisions without

Two of the seven women ordained as Catholic priests in June 2002 carry a caricature of Pope John Paul II to protest the Vatican's stance against women serving as priests. Cardinal Ratzinger, charged in his role with upholding church doctrine, excommunicated the women.

the pope's approval. The two men met every Friday afternoon to discuss all the issues facing the CDF. Ratzinger believed that part of his role was to shield and protect John Paul II from criticism. So, it was Ratzinger who accepted the blame for unpopular rulings. "From the very beginning," he explains, "it was clear to me that during my time in Rome I would have to carry out a lot of unpleasant tasks."[46]

Liberation theology was one of the hot issues that Ratzinger had to deal with. Supporters of liberation theology believe that, in order to help the poor, the church should help groups who want to redistribute wealth by overthrowing governments that oppress the poor.

Liberation theology was especially popular in Latin America where the gap between the rich and poor was great. In fact, some Latin American priests took up arms and joined militant revolutionary groups. And, one priest was killed in armed combat.

To Ratzinger, liberation theology bore a dangerous similarity to Marxism. He felt that liberating the poor was a vital part of the

Pope John Paul II

Karol Wojtyla, the man who would become Pope John Paul II, was born in a small village near Krakow, Poland, in 1920. His mother and two sisters died while he was still a child.

He attended the University of Krakow, where he took part in experimental theater. He then enrolled in the seminary, which the Nazis closed down when they occupied Poland. To avoid being drafted by the Nazis, he hid in the home of the archbishop of Krakow while attending an underground seminary.

Wojtyla became a priest in 1946 and the archbishop of Krakow in 1946. He was an enemy of the communist government that had rose to power in Poland.

In 1978 he was elected pope. His election, and his subsequent visits to Poland, gave courage to people living under communism.

He was an extremely popular pope. He visited more than 115 countries during his reign and spoke eight languages. He was a charming man who enjoyed telling jokes, skiing, and hiking. In 2001 he was diagnosed with Parkinson's disease, which he died of in 2005.

Pope John Paul II blesses visitors in St. Peter's Square. His charm, skill with languages, and tireless travel schedule made him extremely popular among his followers.

church's mission and urged all Catholics to do so, but not through politics or revolution. According to author Greg Watts, "the kind of liberation theology Ratzinger supported could be found in the life of Mother Teresa, an Albanian nun who had gone to live in the slums of Calcutta and set up Missionaries of Charity to care for the poor, the sick and the abandoned."[47]

In response to the threat he felt liberation theology posed, Ratzinger prepared a document condemning liberation theology. And, he censored Brazilian theologian Leonardo Boff, the leader of the liberation theology movement, ordering him to stop teaching and writing about the subject. This did not please supporters of the philosophy who, according to an article in the *New Yorker*, called Ratzinger, "a snapping dog who threatens all dissidents [rebels] with appropriate punishment."[48]

Another controversial issue Ratzinger faced was the ordination of women. In 2002 a radical bishop ordained seven women in Austria. Although other Christian religions allow women to serve as pastors, women have always been prohibited from serving as Catholic priests. Since all of the apostles who assisted Jesus Christ were men, the church believes that only men should serve as priests. Ratzinger's role as prefect was to uphold the church's teachings. He, therefore, affirmed that the seven women had no right to be ordained. The women refused to accept this and insisted the church accept them as priests. As a result, Ratzinger excommunicated the women, who left the Catholic Church to join another Christian sect. Once again, Ratzinger's critics condemned him, labeling him a sexist. However, he did not back down.

Still another group of issues concerned the church's role in an individual's private life. The church views the use of contraception, premarital sex, abortion, and homosexuality as sins. Some Catholics wanted the church to adjust to the times and openly challenged the church's teachings on these issues. Once again, Ratzinger sided with the church.

His rulings on these and many other issues made Ratzinger the target of harsh criticism. His opponents disparaged not just his interpretation of the faith, but also him personally. Despite the personal attacks, he held firm. As always, his loyalty was to the church. He did what he believed was right. Many Catholics were grateful for his leadership. In a 2003 interview with Raymond Arroyo, director of Eternal World Television Network, a Catholic television network, Ratzinger talked about his role as prefect of the CDF. He said:

It's in many senses uncomfortable. We have essentially and often to do with all the problems of the Church. ... Also with disciplinary cases ... we are really in this Congregation confronted with the most difficult aspects of the life of the Church today. And so, also clearly attacked. ... But from the other hand ... everyday I experience that people are thankful saying, "Yes the Church has an identity, has a continuity, the faith is real and present also today and is also today possible." And when I go in St. Peter's Square and so on, I can see everyday people from different parts of the world knowing me and saying, "Thank you, Father. We are thankful that you are doing a difficult job, because this is helping us."[49]

A Simple Life

Ratzinger's life was not easy. He put in a long day that was filled with more than just his prefect duties. In a typical morning, according to author Michael Collins,

he was in the office before eight o'clock. The morning was normally filled with appointments. The first two hours were dedicated to responding to pending correspondence or returning phone calls. By ten o'clock, the first audiences began. These were as varied as they were unpredictable. Bishops in Rome … theologians, foreign dignitaries, scholars, journalists, pilgrims, ex-students, representatives of other Christian denominations or world religions called to see him. The list was endless. By midday these usually ended, allowing him to return to work. As a member of several other Vatican Congregations and committees, there was preparatory work to be done and interminable meetings to attend.[50]

It was not until the afternoon and evening that he could concentrate on his paperwork as prefect.

Ratzinger spent twenty-four years as prefect of the CDF. The difficult and stressful job took a toll on his health. He suffered a small stroke and developed heart problems. He tried to resign twice, but both times Pope John Paul II asked him to stay. And, Ratzinger, who put his duty to the church first, yielded to the pope.

As prefect, Ratzinger could have lived in a fine apartment in the Vatican, but he chose to live modestly with his sister Maria in a small apartment outside the Vatican walls. He maintained a very simple life, which helped him to deal with the stress of his job. Usually he rose at 5 A.M. each morning and said Mass in a little chapel in his apartment. He dressed in plain black robes, and walked to and

Despite his high profile role at the Vatican, Cardinal Ratzinger maintained a simple private life during his years of service under Pope John Paul II.

from his office in the Vatican carrying his briefcase full of work with him. He went home for lunch almost every day, and took a walk around his neighborhood before returning to work. As he walked, he was often seen feeding stray cats, some of whom he took into his home. In the evenings, he practiced the piano and worked on his own writings, producing twelve books. On Saturdays, he and Maria often hiked in the hills around Rome. In the summers, they vacationed in Bavaria where Ratzinger maintained a home, and where the brother and sister spent time with Georg.

In 1991 Maria died. Her death was a great loss to Ratzinger. But it did not stop him from doing his job. It was not a job he had ever wanted, and it took his life in a direction he never expected. But in doing it, Ratzinger helped shape the direction the church would take in the twenty-first century. "I think that I have been able to do something meaningful," he explains. "I am really thankful for the life God has disposed [arranged] and shaped."[51]

Chapter 5

Facing the Future

As leader of the Catholic Church, Pope Benedict XVI is trying to make the world a better place for everyone. He is working hard to bring people of different faiths together, promote world peace, and protect the environment.

A Promising Beginning

Pope Benedict XVI was installed as the 265th pope on April 24, 2005, in an outdoor Mass held before more than 350,000 spectators. His brother Georg was seated near the altar in a place of honor. Delegations from 130 countries and a diverse group of religious leaders were among the invited guests.

In his sermon, which was repeatedly interrupted by applause and cheers, the new pope did not talk about what his program of governance would be, instead he prayed for strength and guidance. He said:

> At this moment, weak servant of God that I am, I must assume this enormous task, which truly exceeds all human capacity. How can I do this? How will I be able to do it? ... I can say with renewed conviction that I am not alone. I do not have to carry alone what in truth I could never carry alone. All the saints of God are there to protect me, to sustain me, and to carry me. And your prayers, my dear friends, your indulgence, your love, your faith and your hope accompany me. ... Dear friends! At this moment there is no need for me to present a program of governance. ... There will be

Pope Benedict XVI waves from his popemobile to a crowd that includes his brother Georg, far right, after his installation Mass in St. Peter's Square in April 2005.

other opportunities to do so. My real program of governance is not to do my own will, not to pursue my own ideas, but to listen together with the whole church, to the word and the will of the Lord, to be guided by him, so that he himself will lead the church in this hour of history.[52]

When the Mass was over, the new pope received the symbols of his office. The first was a woolen shawl, known as a pallium, and the second was a fisherman's ring. But he refused to put another papal emblem, the papal crown, on his official coat of arms, a shield with important symbols that represent a person's rank and title. Benedict XVI did not see himself as a king, but rather as a simple man doing God's work.

His humility was seen again when the new pope rode through St. Peter's Square in the "pope mobile," a specially designed car that popes use to travel in. Pope Benedict XVI insisted on using an open-topped vehicle so that he would not be separated from the people that filled the square. His words and actions endeared him to his followers.

Building Bridges

In the next few days, Pope Benedict XVI mapped out his plan of governance. Spiritually, he would uphold the traditional values that he believed reflected the church's teachings. In his role as a world leader, he would try to improve relations between the church and other religions, work for peace, and help to create a better world.

In keeping with his plan, Pope Benedict XVI has made continuing efforts to reach out to different world religions. The Catholic Church has not always had the best relations with other religious groups. Therefore, this is an important step in building tolerance and understanding, which should help protect Catholics from acts of violence in countries where they are the religious minority. It should also make the world a more peaceful place for everyone.

In speaking to a group of Muslim leaders, Pope Benedict XVI put it this way:

Peace is also a duty to which all peoples must be committed, especially those who profess to belong to religious traditions. Our efforts to come together and foster dialogue are a valuable contribution to building peace on solid foundations. It is, therefore, imperative to engage in authentic and sincere dialogue, built on respect for the dignity of every human person. ... I assure you that the Church wants to continue building bridges of friendship with followers of all

Upholding Traditional Values

Besides dealing with global issues, Pope Benedict XVI has worked hard to continue fostering traditional values among the world's Catholics. This includes defending and praising traditional families, encouraging charitable acts, and emphasizing the importance of hope and love.

As of early 2008, the pope had issued two encyclicals. These are letters from the pope sent to all the bishops in the church. The theme of the first is love. In it, the pope discusses how important it is for humans to see their connection to each other, to love and help one another, and to love God. Part of loving and helping one another involves giving charity to the needy. Serving as a role model, Pope Benedict XVI was one of the first people to buy a bond issued by the British government in 2007. The money raised by the bond is being used to provide vaccinations for children in undeveloped countries.

The pope's second encyclical's theme is hope. In it, Pope Benedict XVI emphasizes how religious faith gives people hope even in the worst of times and carries them forward. The pope trusts that his words will give strength to those who are suffering.

religions, in order to seek the true good of every person and of society as a whole.[53]

Success from Failure

Some of the pope's efforts toward building interreligion understanding have been more successful than others. One, a lecture he gave at the University of Regensburg to a group of theologians on September 12, 2006, caused problems. In the lecture he quoted a fifteenth-century Christian Byzantine emperor who implied that the Muslim religion sanctions violence. The statement was part of a larger speech, which dealt with the need to balance faith and reason. It was not meant to slur Islam.

In an article in *Time* magazine, authors David Van Biema and Jeff Israely explain the essence of the speech in this way:

> His vehicle was a talk about reason as part of Christianity's very essence. His nominal target was … the secular [nonreligious] West, which he said had committed the tragic error of discarding Christianity as reason-free. The pope then went on to compare this to Islam, which he said actually did undervalue rationality, and which he … suggested was consequently more inclined to violence.[54]

The statement caused an intense reaction in the Muslim world. Middle Eastern newspapers blasted the pope. Figures of him were burned in effigy. The Moroccan ambassador was withdrawn from

Protesters in Jerusalem denounce Pope Benedict XVI in September 2006, one of many such demonstrations across the Muslim world after the pope delivered a speech that some people interpreted as critical of Islam.

the Vatican. The chief Muslim leader in Somalia urged his fellow Muslims to hunt Pope Benedict XVI down and kill him, and a novel portraying the murder of the pope became a best seller in Turkey. Worse yet, churches throughout the Middle East were vandalized, priests were attacked, and a nun in Somalia was slain.

Over the course of the next few weeks, Pope Benedict XVI took a number of steps to repair the damage. According to Van Biema and Israely, "he expressed regret to those offended, summoned a group of Muslim notables to make the point personally and disowned the ... slur ... as Manuel's [the fifteenth-century emperor] sentiment and not his own. He even issued a second version of the speech to reflect those sentiments."[55] No other pope had ever done these things.

Moreover, despite all the controversy and threats of violence, Pope Benedict XVI refused to cancel a previously scheduled trip to Turkey, a predominately Muslim nation, set for November 2006. "To hold firm to his resolve to visit Turkey in the face of this turmoil showed exceptional courage and trust in providence [God],"[56] explains religion writer Drew Christiansen.

Once in Turkey, Pope Benedict XVI proved to the world just how serious he was about building connections between the world's religions when he visited the Blue Mosque, one of Islam's most religious sites. He was the second pope ever to enter a Muslim house of worship and the first to actually pray in a mosque.

Standing beside Istanbul's Grand Mufti, the city's highest Islamic leader, Pope Benedict XVI faced toward Mecca, the holy city that Muslims face toward when they pray, and he prayed. In the many centuries of church history, no other pope had ever prayed in a mosque before. The pope's action was seen as a sign of respect for Islam and was well received throughout the Muslim world. According to the Grand Mufti, Mustafa Cagrici, that action was, "more meaningful than an apology."[57]

The pope also made gains in bringing Catholics and Muslims closer through the speeches he made during his visit. He said,

The best way forward is via authentic dialogue between Christians and Muslims, based on truth and inspired by a sincere wish to know one another better, respecting differences and recognizing what we have in common. ... Our

Pope Benedict XVI stands with Muslim clerics and prelates inside the Blue Mosque in Istanbul, Turkey, in November 2006. During his visit, he faced the holy city of Mecca to pray, as is the practice of followers of Islam.

world must come to realize that all people are linked by profound solidarity with one another, and they must be encouraged to assert their historical and cultural differences.[58]

Benedict XVI's trip to Turkey not only helped eased tensions caused by the pope's Regensburg address, it also opened the lines of communication between Catholics and Muslims.

Other Connections

The pope's visit to Turkey was also an important step in improving relations between Catholics and Orthodox Christians. The two groups, which once formed one church, have been at odds since they split in 1054. While in Turkey, Benedict XVI met with and worshipped with Patriarch Barthlomew, the head of the Orthodox Church in Turkey. At the close of their meetings, the two religious leaders issued a joint statement in which they pledged to work toward restoring unity between the two churches.

Pope Benedict XVI is greeted by members of a synagogue in Cologne, Germany, where he also attended services and prayed at a memorial dedicated to Holocaust victims as part of an August 2005 visit to his home country.

In another attempt to open dialogue with other religions, in 2006 the pope met with the Dalai Lama, the spiritual leader of the nation of Tibet. And, following the path that Pope John Paul II had blazed, Pope Benedict XVI has also reached out to the Jewish people.

The pope, who grew up in Nazi Germany, is particularly sensitive to the suffering that the Holocaust caused the Jewish people. In 2005 he visited a synagogue in Cologne, Germany, that had been rebuilt after being destroyed by the Nazis. Inside the synagogue, he stopped and prayed silently before a memorial dedicated to the eleven thousand Jews of Cologne who were killed during the Holocaust. Then he sat silently through the religious service, bowing his head respectively. Pope Benedict XVI was the second pope in history to enter a synagogue. Jews everywhere applauded his actions. "If someone had told me 45 years ago, 'You are going to be in Cologne and the pope will visit you in a synagogue.' I wouldn't have believed it. We have come a long way in mutual support and mutual understanding,"[59] says German Jewish leader, Paul Spiegel.

When the services ended, the pope addressed the congregation. He talked about the Holocaust, the danger of anti-Semitism (hatred of the Jews), and the need for Jews and Catholics to come together. He explained:

> The history of relations between the Jewish and Christian communities has been complex and often painful. There have been blessed times when the two lived peacefully, but there was also ... the darkest period of German and European history ... [which] gave rise to the attempt ... to exterminate European Jewry. ... The terrible events of that time must never cease to rouse consciences, to resolve conflicts, to inspire the building of peace. ... The Catholic Church is committed—I reaffirm this again today—to tolerance, respect, friendship, and peace between all peoples, cultures, and religions. ... Much progress has been made, in Germany, and throughout the world, towards better and closer relations between Jews and Christians. ... Yet much still remains to be done. We must come to know one another much more and much better. Consequently, I would encourage sincere and trustful dialogue between Jews and Christians. ... This dialogue, if it

is sincere, must not gloss over or underestimate the existing differences ... and indeed, precisely in those areas, we need to show respect and love for one another. ... So that, never again will the forces of evil come to power, and that future generations, with God's help, may be able to build a more just and peaceful world, in which all people have equal rights and are equally at home.[60]

A Peacemaker

Besides trying to make peace between the church and other religions, Pope Benedict XVI has taken center stage in trying to bring peace to the world at large. He has done this through his prayers and his actions. For instance, he has supported the Spirit

Pope Benedict XVI's Favorite Things

Like any other individual, Pope Benedict XVI has favorite foods and activities. He loves the food of his native Bavaria, and one of his German friends brings him Bavarian sausages from his homeland. The pope also has a sweet tooth. He loves desserts and fresh honey. In his home in Bavaria, Pope Benedict XVI keeps bees. He also has a golden retriever and a pet cat there. A caretaker who lives on the property looks after the animals.

Although he loves his dog, the pope's favorite animal is the cat. He welcomes stray cats into the Vatican gardens, where he feeds and pets them. Before Pope Benedict XVI's reign, cats were not allowed into the garden.

To relax, the pope reads, plays the piano, and listens to music. His favorite music is that of Mozart. He also enjoys liturgical music, the music played during religious services. He can often be seen listening to music on his iPod.

Among Pope Benedict's favorite pastimes is playing the piano, which he is shown here doing while still serving as a cardinal.

of Assisi, large interreligious pray gatherings dedicated to world peace. And, even before the world community stepped in, Pope Benedict XVI called for a cease-fire and a negotiated settlement to the 2006 Israel-Hezbollah war in Lebanon. He condemned the United States's invasion of Iraq. And, he has repeatedly prayed for peace in Afghanistan, Iraq, Colombia, Sri Lanka, the Congo, Somalia, Ethiopia, and the Sudan, asking that the leaders in these nations be given "the wisdom and courage to seek and find humane, just and lasting solutions."[61]

World peace is so important to Pope Benedict XVI that under his supervision the Vatican has launched a Web site where news of the Vatican's work on justice and peace can be viewed.

The pope is not just concerned with peace now. He is also concerned with the future. With that in mind, he has spoken out in support of nuclear disarmament, the elimination of all nuclear weapons. In 2006 he stated:

> What can be said, too, about those governments which count on nuclear arms as a means of ensuring the security of their countries? Along with countless persons of good will, one can state that this point of view is not only baneful [bad] but also completely fallacious [untrue]. In a nuclear war there would be no victors, only victims. The truth of peace requires that all—whether those governments which openly or secretly possess nuclear arms, or those planning to acquire them—agree to change their course by clear and firm decisions, and strive for a progressive and concerted nuclear disarmament. The resources, which would be saved, could then be employed in projects of development capable of benefiting all their people, especially the poor. ... It can only be hoped that the international community will find the wisdom and courage to take up once more, jointly and with renewed conviction, the process of disarmament, and thus concretely ensure the right to peace enjoyed by every individual and every people.[62]

Protecting the Environment

Another way the pope has been working to make the world a better place is by taking steps to help protect the environment. The pope believes that caring for all creation, including the earth, is everyone's duty. Moreover, he thinks that when humans abuse the earth and deplete its natural resources, the ensuing shortages lead to conflicts and wars.

With this in mind, Pope Benedict XVI has taken steps to make Vatican City the first independent, carbon-neutral state in the world. Being carbon neutral means balancing the amount of carbon released into the atmosphere with renewable energy that releases an equal amount of nonpolluting usable energy. To do this, the pope has commissioned the building of more than one thousand solar panels on the roof of the Vatican's Paul VI audience hall. The panels, which cover an area as large as a football field,

An advocate for environmental awareness and protection, Pope Benedict XVI donned a green robe to celebrate Mass at a Vatican-sponsored eco-friendly youth rally as part of Italy's annual Save Creation Day celebrations in September 2007.

will produce enough electricity to light, cool, and heat the entire building. The panels are to be installed sometime in 2008. If the panels prove to be effective, the project may be expanded.

Another part of the pope's effort to make the Vatican a carbon-neutral state involves the planting of trees in a national park in Hungary. Known as the Vatican Climate Forest, the new forest should produce enough oxygen to counterbalance the Vatican's carbon dioxide emissions. This is important because carbon dioxide emissions are linked to global warming.

The pope is also working to spread awareness of environmental issues among young people. In 2007, as part of the Italian church's annual Save Creation Day, he sponsored the church's first eco-friendly youth rally. About a half million young people attended the two-day rally. The Vatican issued all the participants special environmentally friendly kits, which included backpacks made of recycled material, prayer books printed on recycled paper, hand crank flashlights that work without batteries, and color-coded trash bags, which allowed the participants to separate their personal trash for recycling. The kits not only made the participants more aware of ways to help the environment, but also resulted in less litter and damage to the rally site than in the past.

To symbolize the importance of taking care of the earth, the pope conducted Sunday Mass at the rally dressed in a green robe. Then he spoke to the young crowd, explaining that the future of the earth was in their hands, saying:

> Dear young people … There is no doubt that one of the fields in which it seems urgent to take action is that of safeguarding creation. The future of the planet is entrusted to the new generations, in which there are evident signs of a development that has not always been able to protect the delicate balances of nature. Before it is too late, it is necessary to make courageous decisions that can recreate a strong alliance between humankind and the earth. A decisive "yes" is needed to protect creation.[63]

It is clear that Pope Benedict XVI is working hard to protect all of creation. He is doing so, while sharing his hope, faith, and

Pope Benedict XVI stands at Ground Zero during a visit to the United States in April 2008 to greet the families of victims of the September 11, 2001, terrorist attacks on the World Trade Center.

love with his followers. In April 2008 he visited the United States. He met with President George W. Bush, addressed the United Nations, prayed with the relatives of 9/11 victims at Ground Zero, and celebrated Mass in Washington D.C.'s National Stadium and New York's Yankee Stadium. In his quiet and humble way, this gentle scholar is leading the Catholic Church forward, and with each step he hopes to make the world a better place. "He seems to have received a great gift enabling him to do this incredibly difficult job that was thrust upon him," says Archbishop William Levada. "And in doing it, to radiate serenity and joy."[64]

Notes

Introduction: A New Pope

1. Quoted in Associated Press, "One Year Later Remembering Pope John Paul II," MSNBC, April 8, 2005, www.msnbc.msn. com/id/3305285.
2. CNN.com, "European Press Hails New Pope," CNN.com, April 20, 2005, www.cnn.com/2005/WORLD/europe/04/20/ pope.press/index.html.
3. Quoted in CNN.com, "European Press Hails New Pope."
4. Quoted in CBS News, "Benedict: I Prayed Not to Be Pope," CBS News, April 25, 2005, www.cbsnews.com/stories/2005/04/02/ world/main684865.shtml.
5. Quoted in CNN.com, "Catholics React to the Announcement of New Pope," CNN.com, April 19, 2005, www.cnn.com/ 2005/WORLD/europe/04/19/pope.catholic.react/index. html.
6. Richard P. McBrien, "The New Benedict Must Choose His Path," *National Catholic Reporter*, May 6, 2005.
7. Quoted in Greg Watts, *Labourer in the Vineyard*. Oxford, England: Lion, 2005, p. 16.

Chapter 1: Church and Family

8. Joseph Ratzinger, *Milestones*. San Francisco, CA: Ignatius, 1998, p. 8.
9. Quoted in Felicity Dargan, "My Cousin the Pope," Cultural Catholic, www.culturalcatholic.com/PopeCousin.htm.
10. Ratzinger, *Milestones*, p. 17.
11. Ratzinger, *Milestones*, p. 18.
12. Quoted in Mark Lander and Richard Bernstein, "A Future Pope Is Recalled: A Lover of Cats and Mozart, Dazzled by the Church as a Boy," NYTimes.com, April 22, 2005, www.nytimes. com/2005/04/22/international/worldspecial2/22germany. html?ei=5088&en=deb8ac4c18fa6d14&ex=1271822400& partner=rssnyt&emc=rss&pagewanted=all&position=.

13. Joseph Cardinal Ratzinger, *Salt of the Earth*. San Francisco, CA: Ignatius, 1997, p. 52.
14. Ratzinger, *Milestones*, p. 14.
15. Ratzinger, *Milestones*, p. 19.
16. Ratzinger, *Salt of the Earth*, p. 45.
17. Ratzinger, *Milestones*, p. 25.
18. Ratzinger, *Milestones*, p. 27.

Chapter 2: A Reluctant Warrior

19. Quoted in *USA Today*, "New Pope Defied Nazis as Teen During WWII," *USA Today*, April 23, 2005, www.usatoday.com/news/world/2005-04-23-new-pope-defied-Nazis_x.htm.
20. Quoted in Associated Press, "Jews Concerned as Germanic Hardliner, Ex-Hitler Youth Elected Pope," Israel Insider, April 19, 2005, http://web.israelinsider.com/Articles/Diplomacy/5354.htm.
21. Quoted in Michael Kress, "What Joseph Ratzinger Did During the War," Beliefnet, www.beliefnet.com/story/165/story_16547.html.
22. Ratzinger, *Salt of the Earth*, p. 32.
23. Michael Collins, *Pope Benedict XVI*. Mahwah, NJ: Paulist, 2005, p. 16.
24. Ratzinger, *Milestones*, p. 33.
25. Ratzinger, *Milestones*, p. 34.
26. Quoted in *USA Today*, "New Pope Defied Nazis as Teen During WWII."
27. Ratzinger, *Milestones*, p. 36.
28. Ratzinger, *Salt of the Earth*, p. 58.
29. Ratzinger, *Milestones*, p. 40.

Chapter 3: Priest and Scholar

30. Watts, *Labourer in the Vineyard*, p. 24.
31. Ratzinger, *Salt of the Earth*, p. 55.
32. Ratzinger, *Salt of the Earth*, p. 53.
33. Ratzinger, *Milestones*, p. 99.
34. Ratzinger, *Salt of the Earth*, p. 63.
35. Collins, *Pope Benedict XVI*, p. 33.

36. Quoted in Collins, *Pope Benedict XVI*, p. 33.
37. Joseph Cardinal Ratzinger with Vittorio Messori, *The Ratzinger Report*. San Francisco, CA: Ignatius, 1985, p. 18.
38. Quoted in Watts, *Labourer in the Vineyard*, p. 34.
39. Quoted in Gianni Valente, "The Difficult Years," *30 Days*, www.30giorni.it/us/articolo_stampa.asp?id=10525.
40. Quoted in Richard Bernstein, Daniel J. Wakin, Mark Landler, and Christus Rex, "Turbulence on Campus in 60's Hardened Views of Future Pope, *New York Times*, April 25, 2005, www.christusrex.org/www1/news/nyt-4-25-05d.html.

Chapter 4: Protector of the Faith

41. Ratzinger, *Salt of the Earth*, p. 81.
42. Ratzinger, *Milestones*, p. 152.
43. Ratzinger, *Salt of the Earth*, p. 85.
44. Eternal World Television Network, "Some Quotations from His Books," Eternal World Television Network, www.ewtn.com/pope/words/some_quotations.asp.
45. Vatican Web site, "Congregation for the Doctrine of the Faith," Vatican Web site, www.vatican.va/roman_curia/congregations/cfaith/documents/rc_con_cfaith_pro_14071997_en.html.
46. Ratzinger, *Salt of the Earth*, p. 83.
47. Watts, *Labourer in the Vineyard*, p. 47.
48. Andy Grafton, "Reading Ratzinger," *New Yorker*, July 25, 2005, p. 42.
49. Eternal World Television Network, "The World Over: Cardinal Ratzinger Interview," Eternal World Television Network, www.ewtn.com/library/issues/ratzintv.htm.
50. Collins, *Pope Benedict XVI*, p. 82.
51. Ratzinger, *Salt of the Earth*, p. 117.

Chapter 5: Facing the Future

52. Catholic News Service, "Text of Pope Benedict XVI's Homily at Installation Mass," Catholic News Service, April 24, 2005, www.catholicnews.com/data/stories/cns/0502556.htm.
53. Quoted in CBS News, "Benedict, I Prayed Not to Be Pope," CBS News, April 25, 2005, www.cbsnews.com/stories/2005/04/02/world/main684865.shtml.

54. David Van Biema and Jeff Israely, "The Passion of the Pope," *Time*, November 27, 2006, p. 40.
55. Van Biema and Israely, "The Passion of the Pope," p. 40.
56. Drew Christiansen, "Benedict XVI: Peacemaker," *America*, July 16, 2007, p. 10.
57. Quoted in David Willey, "Turkey Trip Defines Benedict Papacy," BBC News, December 1, 2006, http://news.bbc.co.uk/go/pr/fr/-/1/hi/world/europe/6199350.stm.
58. Quoted in CNN News, "Pope Calls for Christian-Muslim Dialogue," CNN News, November 28, 2006, www.cnn.com/2006/WORLD/europe/11/28/turkey.pope/index.html?section=cnn_latest.
59. Quoted in Ian Fisher, "Benedict Visits Cologne Synagogue," *International Herald Tribune*, August 20, 2005, www.iht.com/articles/2005/08/19/news/pope.php.
60. Benedict XVI, "Address of his Holiness Pope Benedict XVI," speech given at the Synagogue of Cologne, August 19, 2005, Vatican Web site, www.vatican.va/holy_father/benedict_xvi/speeches/2005/august/documents/hf_ben-xvi_spe_20050819_cologne-synagogue_en.html.
61. MSNBC, "Pope Makes Christmas Day Appeal," MSNBC, December 25, 2007, www.msnbc.msn.com/id/22390769.
62. Benedict XVI, "Message of His Holiness Pope Benedict XVI for the Celebration of the World Day of Peace," January 1, 2006, Vatican Web site, www.vatican.va/holy_father/benedict_xvi/messages/peace/documents/hf_ben-xvi_mes_20051213_xxxix-world-day-peace_en.html.
63. Benedict XVI, "Homily of His Holiness Benedict XVI," September 2, 2007, Vatican Web site, www.vatican.va/holy_father/benedict_xvi/homilies/2007/documents/hf_ben-xvi_hom_20070902_loreto_en.html.
64. Quoted in Russell Shaw, "Our Quiet Pope," Catholic.com, www.catholic.com/thisrock/2006/0604fea1.asp.

1927

Joseph Alois Ratzinger was born on April 16, 1927, in Marktl am Inn, Germany.

1929

The Ratzinger family moves to Tittmoning.

1932

The family moves to Aschau am Inn.

1937

The family moves to Traunstein, which becomes their permanent home.

1939

Ratzinger enrolls in St. Michael's seminary in Traunstein. World War II begins.

1941

Ratzinger is forced to enroll in Hitler Youth.

1942

Georg Ratzinger is drafted.

1943

Ratzinger is drafted into the Flak.

1944

Ratzinger is drafted into the labor service branch of the German army.

1945

Ratzinger deserts the army. World War II ends. Ratzinger is taken prisoner of war by the Allies. Ratzinger enters the seminary in Freising.

1947

Ratzinger enters the Theological Institute of the University of Munich.

1951

Ratzinger is ordained as a priest.

1953

Ratzinger receives his doctoral degree.

1957

Ratzinger receives a second advanced degree, which qualifies him to be a professor in a German university.

1958

Ratzinger becomes a professor at the University of Munich.

1959

Ratzinger becomes a professor at the University of Bonn. His father dies.

1962

Ratzinger serves as an adviser to Cardinal Frings for Vatican II. He serves on Vatican II through 1965.

1963

Ratzinger's mother dies.

1966

Ratzinger becomes a professor at the University of Turbingen.

1968

Student uprisings rock the University of Turbingen and disrupt Ratzinger's classes.

1969

Ratzinger becomes a professor at the University of Regensburg.

1977

Ratzinger is named archbishop of Munich and Freising on March 14. He is made a cardinal on June 27. Pope Paul VI dies. Pope John Paul dies. Pope John Paul II becomes pope.

1981

Ratzinger is named prefect of the Congregation of Faith by Pope John Paul II. He holds this position until 2005.

1991

Ratzinger's sister, Maria, dies.

2005

Pope John Paul II dies. Ratzinger becomes the new pope, Benedict XVI.

For More Information

Books

Clifford W. Mills, *Pope Benedict XVI*. New York: Chelsea House, 2007. A biography of the pope's life.

Jeanne Perego, *Joseph and Chico: A Cat Tells the Life of Pope Benedict XVI*. San Francisco, CA: Ignatius Press, 2008. This picture book is an authorized biography of the pope told by Chico, the pope's former cat. Although geared to children, young adults will appreciate the interesting facts and illustrations.

Joseph Ratzinger, *Milestones*. San Francisco, CA: Ignatius Press, 1998. The pope's autobiography covering his life from 1927 to 1977.

Tom Streissguth, *Pope Benedict XVI*. Minneapolis, MN: Twenty-First Century Books, 2007. A biography of the pope's life.

Periodicals

Drew Christiansen, "Benedict XVI: Peacemaker," *America*, July 16, 2007.

Nancy Gibbs, "The New Shepherd," *Time*, May 2, 2005.

USA Today, "New Pope Defied Nazis as Teen During WWII," April 23, 2005.

David Van Biema and Jeff Israely, "The Passion of the Pope," *Time*, November 27, 2006.

Web Sites

The Cardinal Ratzinger Fan Club (www.ratzingerfanclub. com). This Web site offers copies of some of Cardinal Ratzinger's writings, information about his position on the CDC, and biographical information.

Eternal World Television Network (www.ewtn.com). This Web site offers biographical information, information about the pope's coat of arms and about the name Pope Benedict.

PopeBenedictthe16th.com (www.popebenedictthe16th.com). This site offers articles, photos, and biographical information on Pope Benedict XVI and provides links for more information.

The Pope Benedict XVI Fan Club (www.popebenedictxvifan club.com). This site offers all sorts of information about the pope, including interviews and articles about him and a collection of his writing.

Vatican Web Site (www.vatican.va). This fascinating Web site has information on the pope, copies of all his speeches and homilies, and information on the Vatican, including a virtual tour and a link to the Pontifical Council for Justice and Peace.

A

Animals, 84
Apostolic Palace (Vatican), 66
Archbishop of Munich and
    Freising, 59–61, *60*
Arroyo, Raymond, 72
Aschau am Inn, Germany, 20

B

Baptism, 15, *16*
Barthlomew, Patriarch of
    Orthodox Church, 82
Bavaria
    about, 21
    childhood, 14–15, 17–18, 21
    food, 84
    importance of Catholicism, 15
Bavarian Motor Works (BMW),
    30
Benedict XV (pope), 11
    environment, 86, 87, 88
Benedict XVI (pope), *81*
    chosen as name, 11–12
    favorite foods and activities,
        84, *85*
    greeting crowds after election,
        12
    installation as pope, 75–77, *76*
    nuclear disarmament, 85–86
    on nuclear disarmament, 86
    on relations with other reli-
        gions, 77–78, 80, 82, 83–84
    See also Ratzinger, Joseph Alois
Blue Mosque (Istanbul), 80, *81*
Boff, Leonardo, 71
Bonn, University of, 50–51
Bush, George W., 89

C

Cagrici, Mustafa, 80
Carbon neutrality, 86, 88
Cardinals
    Ratzinger, Joseph Alois made,
        61
    selection of pope, 10–11,
        61–62, 63
Cathedral of Our Lady
    (Munich), 61
Catholic Church
    clergy as victims of Nazis, 20, 37
    divisions within, 11, 53, 69, 72
    First Vatican Council, 51
    Hitler and, 37
    importance to Ratzinger
        family, 15, 18
    liturgy, 21–23, 53, 84
    priesthood preparation,
        25–26, 42–43, 45
    relations with other religions,
        77–80, *81*, 82–85
    role of pastor, 46–47
    Second Vatican Council, 51,
        52, 53, 63, 68
    traditional values, 78
    Vatican, *64–65*, 66, 86, 88
Charity as traditional Catholic
    value, 78
Childhood
    favorite home during, 23
    importance of Catholic
        Church, 15, 18
    importance of siblings, 17–18
    music during, 19
    religious education, 21
Children and Ratzinger, Joseph

Alois, 46–47, *60*, 78, 88
Christiansen, Drew, 80
Church of Precious Blood, 46–48
College of Cardinals, 10, 61–62, 63
Collins, Michael, 33, 50–51, 73
Communio (journal), 43
Concentration camps, 28, 30, 32, 37
Conclave of the Sacred College of Cardinals, 10, 61–62, 63
Congregation for the Doctrine of the Faith (CDF)
  controversial issues before, 68–73
  John Paul II and, 66–67
  life as prefect, 73–74
  modernized, 53
  prefect, 8, *9*, 67–70, 72–74

D
Dachau (concentration camp), 30
Dahm, Volker, 28–39
Dalai Lama, 83

E
Education
  advanced degrees, 48–49
  Nazis and, 20–21, 37
  pre-seminary, 23–24
  for priesthood, 25–26, 42–43, 45
  Ratzinger, Joseph Alois as teacher, 45, 48, *50*, 56–57
Encyclicals, 78
Environment, 86, *87*, 88
Essay contest, 45–46

F
Faulhaber, Michael, 18, 46
The final solution, 32
First Vatican Council, 51

The Flak, 30, *31*, 32
Foods, 84
France and social revolution, *54–55*, 56
Freising archbishop, 59–61, *60*
Freising seminary, 42–43
Frings, Cardinal of Cologne, 51

G
Germany
  after World War I, 18, 20
  Hitler Youth, 28–30, *29*
  during World War II, 26, 30, 32, 33, 36
  See also Bavaria; Nazi Party
Gymnasium, 24

H
Habilitations, 49
Health, 73
Hebblethwaite, Peter, 53
Hitler, Adolf
  Catholic Church and, 37
  education and, 20–21
  Jews and, 30, 32–33
  rise to power, 20
Hitler Youth, 28–30, *29*
Holocaust, understanding, 30, 82, 84
Hope as traditional Catholic value, 78
Hungary, 33, 88

I
Introduction to Christianity (Ratzinger, Joseph Alois), 57
Iraq, 85
Islam, relations with, 77–80, *79*, *81*, 82
Israel-Hezbollah war (2006), 85
Israely, Jeff, *79*, 80

J
Jews
  Benedict XVI and, 82, 83–84
  Nazis and, 30, 32–33
John Paul I (pope), 63
John Paul II (pope), 62, 71
  background, 63, 70
  continuation of legacy, 10
  death, 8, 70
  Jews and, 83–84
  Ratzinger, Joseph Alois and, 9,
    62–63, 66–70
John XXIII (pope), 51, 59

K
Kasper, Walter, 11
Kopp, Erika (cousin), 15, 17

L
Latin America, 70
Lebanon war (2006), 85
Levada, William, 89
Liberation theology, 70–72
Liturgy, 21–23, 53, 84
Love as traditional Catholic
  value, 78
Luciani, Albino, 63

M
Magnum silencium (rule of
  silence), 43
Marktl am Inn, Germany, 14,
  14–15, 22
Marxism, 57, 70
Mass, 47, 48, 53
McBrien, Richard P., 11–12
Messori, Vittorio, 53
Moll, Helmut, 56–57
Mother Teresa, 71
Munich, University of, 43, 45,
  49

Munich archbishop, 59–61, 60
Music, 18, 84, 85
Muslims, relations with, 77–80,
  79, 81, 82

N
National Catholic Reporter
  (newspaper), 11–12
National Socialist Party. *See* Nazi
  Party
Nazi Party, 19
  attacks on clergy, 20, 37
  education and, 20–21, 37
  employment and, 23
  Jews and, 30, 32–33
  membership, 20
  resistance to, 28–30, 36–38
New Yorker (magazine), 71–72
1960s social revolution, 56
Nuclear disarmament, 85–86

O
Orthodox Christian Church, 82

P
Papal name selection, 11–12
Paul VI (pope), 59, 61
Peace efforts, 84–85
Petrosillo, Otazio, 10–11
Pius XI (pope), 37, 39
Poetry, 43
Pope mobile, 76, 77
Popes
  encyclicals, 78
  installation, 75–77
  name selection, 11–12
  selection by cardinals, 10–11,
    61–62, 63
  symbols of office, 76–77
"Pope's Enforcer," 8
Prisoners of war (POWs), 38, 40

Privacy matters and Catholic
  Church, 72

R
Ratzinger, Georg (brother)
  on brother's desire to be
    cardinal, 18
  childhood, 15
  as choir director, 49–50
  drafted, 27
  in family portraits, 24, 47
  at installation of brother as
    pope, 75, 76
  music and, 18
  ordination, 46
  at Saint Michael's Seminary,
    24–26
  during World War II, 41
Ratzinger, Joseph Alois
  on academic theology, 45
  on acceptance of papacy, 12
  on baptism with holy Easter
    water, 15, 16
  on becoming archbishop,
    60–61
  on being CDF prefect, 8, 67–
    70, 72–73
  birth, 14
  as cardinal, 67
  celebrating Mass, 47, 48
  childhood, 15, 17–19, 21, 23
  on day Hitler came to power,
    20
  desertion, 36–37
  in family portraits, 24, 47
  on father's opposition to
    Nazis, 20
  health, 73
  on his guardian angel, 38
  on home in Traunstein, 23
  importance of Catholicism,

15, 18, 32
  on John Paul II, 8, 63
  on life at Saint Michaels'
    Seminary, 26
  on love of Catholic liturgy,
    21–23
  love of scholarship, 23, 51
  on meaningfulness of his life, 74
  opposition to Nazis, 28–30, 38
  on ordination as archbishop, 61
  ordination as priest, 46
  personal desires, 11
  personality, 8, 10, 13, 53, 77
  on teaching, 45
  on World War II
    bombings, 30, 32
    end of war in Europe, 40
    experience with SS, 33
    family surviving, 41
    returning home from
      Hungary, 36
  See also Benedict XVI (pope)
Ratzinger, Joseph (father),
  14–15, 17
  in family portraits, 24, 47
  Nazi Party and, 20, 23, 38
  when elderly, 49–50
Ratzinger, Maria (mother), 14–
  15, 17, 23
  in family portraits, 24, 47
  when elderly, 49–50
Ratzinger, Maria (sister)
  brother's tuition, 25
  childhood, 15
  death, 74
  in family portraits, 24, 47
  help with habilitation, 49
  in Rome, 73, 74
Regensburg, University of, 43, 58
Rudin, A. James, 30
Rule of silence, 43

S

Sacred College of Cardinals, 10, 61–62, 63

Saint Augustine, 45–46

Saint Benedict of Nursia, 11

Saint Bonaventure, 49

Saint Michael's Seminary, 25, 25–26

Salt of the Earth (Ratzinger, Joseph Alois), 44

Save Creation Day, 87, 88

Scholarship
advanced degrees, 48–49
in gymnasium, 24
of John Paul II, 63
love of, 23, 51
loyalty to Catholic Church vs., 11
monasteries and, 11
in seminary, 42–43

Seckler, Max, 57

Second Vatican Council, 51, 52, 53, 63, 68

Seminaries, 25, 25–26, 42–43

Slave labor, 30

Social revolution, 54–55, 56, 57–58

Spiegel, Paul, 83

Spirit of Assisi, 84–85

Sports, 26

SS officers, 33, 37–38

St. Peter's Basilica (Vatican), 64–65

La Stampa (newspaper), 10

Student rebellions, 56, 57–58

T

30 Days (journal), 56–57

Time (magazine), 79

Tittmoning, Germany, 17–18

Traunstein, Germany, 23–27, 34–35, 36, 40–41

Tubingen, University of, 53, 56–58

Turkey, 80, 82

U

United Nations, 89

United States and social revolution, 56

United States visit, 89

University life, 43, 45

V

Valente, Gianni, 56–57

Van Biema, David, 79, 80

Vatican, 64–65, 66, 86, 88

Vatican Climate Forest, 88

Vatican II, 51, 52, 53, 63, 68

W

Watts, Greg, 42–43, 71

Wojtyla, Karol. *See* John Paul II (pope)

Women priests, 69, 72

World War II
conversion of Saint Michaels' Seminary to hospital, 26
destruction, 33, 36
draft, 27, 30
ended in Europe, 40
the Flak, 30, 31, 32
prisoners of war, 38, 40

Writings
essay contest, 45–46
Introduction to Christianity, 57
paper on Saint Bonaventure, 49
Salt of the Earth, 44
variety, 43

Picture Credits

Cover: Image copyright Michal Mrozek, 2008. Used under license from Shutterstock.com

AP Images, 12, 14, 24, 25, 31, 44, 47, 48, 50, 60, 62, 67, 69, 76, 79, 81, 82, 85, 89

Carlo Bavagnoli/Time & Life Pictures/Getty Images, 52, 54–55

© Bettmann/Corbis, 9

Giuseppe Cacace/Getty Images, 87

Grzegorz Galazka/Getty Images, 74

Heinrich Hoffmann/Time & Life Pictures/Getty Images, 29

Image copyright Mirec, 2008. Used under license from Shutterstock.com, 64–65

Joerg Koch/AFP/Getty Images, 16

John Macdougall/AFP/Getty Images, 22, 34–35

Popperfoto/Getty Images, 19,

James L. Stanfield/National Geographic/Getty Images, 71

Topical Press Agency/Hulton Archive/Getty Images, 39

About the Author

Barbara Sheen is the author of more than forty books for young people. She lives in New Mexico with her family. In her spare time she likes to swim, walk, garden, read, and cook.